WHAT IF WE PRAY

7 PRAYER PRINCIPLES FOR ENJOYING GOD

LACEY ROZELL

Joyful Bee
Ministries

Southlake, TX / Lacey Rozell — First Edition

Hardcover ISBN 979-8-9867898-0-4

Paperback ISBN 979-8-9867898-2-8

Ebook ISBN 979-8-9867898-1-1

Cover Art: Becka Gruber | Get Em Tiger

Edited by: Lauren Kahler Simonic | littlefoxesediting.com

Printed in the United States of America

Joyful Bee Ministries | www.laceyrozell.com

For Scott
My husband and best friend.
Thank you for all your support and for always embracing my chaos
with a smile on your face.

Your Free Gift

———

As we begin to embark on your prayer journey throughout this book, I wanted to give you a gift to help along the way:

A Free Weekly Prayer Journal

This free downloadable allows you to write down what you are learning as you are creating a thriving prayer life.

Scan the QR code below for more information:

PRAISE FOR LACEY ROZELL

Lacey Rozell does a spectacular job of calling you to repentance in a gentle and clear way. The examples and stories she gives throughout the book, show a vulnerability and honesty that helps you see no one is above working on themselves. She was also kind enough to give my husband a copy and he loves it!!!

AMAZON.COM READER

More than ever before, We need a prayer life! In this book, "What If We Pray", Lacey puts principles, experiences of Life and just trusting God before us. Showing us how to pray and what it can DO! Amazing Book from an Awesome Writer!

All you need to DO is say YES!!!

RUSSELR: AMAZON.COM READER

So helpful, insightful, thorough, well organized; extensive Bible & life examples.

I was immediately sold just from the introduction..so relatable! Its a wonderful book! Thankful & eager to continue learning from her insights.

BARBARA: AMAZON.COM READER

CONTENTS

INTRODUCTION

HAVE YOU EVER BEEN DESPERATE?

Walking out of an ER with a catheter bag of my own urine around my ankle was my point of desperation.

In 2014 I found myself in a very desperate situation. I was three months into pregnancy—my fourth in three years—the third that I would carry to term and itching head to toe with a rash. The doctor said an average woman could use topical Benadryl, but I am hardly ever average. As much as I love being an outlier, a medical outlier is not nearly as fun. It means that the medicines that work for most don't work for me...and Benadryl is now on that long list of medicines. You see in less than one percent of people who use Benadryl they can lose the ability to urinate. Yes, you read that correctly. So there I was, three months pregnant with two toddlers under three, covered in scratch marks and doubled over from pain trying to figure out why I couldn't pee. Three babysitters, two doctors and one catheter bag later I was in bed tossing and turning unable to sleep and angry. I was angry that this was another hard pregnancy. I was angry that there was a bag of my own urine hanging next to me. Finally, I was angry at God who promises to give joy to his children in all circumstances yet I was joyless and miserable. I did not have a heart full of joy, I only had a bag full of pee. I was desperate. That led me to a question...a question that started me on the journey that led me here, writing this book today: "What if I pray?"

The title *What if We Pray?* reflects a question I started asking myself that night and have been shocked at the results. This book is my testimony of what I've learned when I have prayed. In Scripture, prayer is what we are shown to do when we are desperate. We see examples of godly people who are desperate and then they pray. Hannah was desperate to have a child, she prayed, and God gave her Samuel—one of the few godly judges of Israel. In fact, Scripture is full of desperate barren women who cried out to God and were able to conceive. Then, during Jesus' ministry many desperate people cried out to Jesus and he healed them. The blind saw, the deaf heard, the bleeding stopped bleeding, the lame walked, the demon possessed were set free—and they all had one thing in common: they were desperate and cried out to God. So what does this tell us about the desperate? That there is no hope? They should give up? Fix themselves?

Nope.

It tells us that God hears the desperate. He wants you to cry out to him when you are desperate. He wants to come to your rescue. When you are desperate, pray to the God who loves you and will never leave you.

Psalm 23:4 tells us exactly what happened to me that night:

> *"Even though I walk through the valley of the shadow of death, I will fear no evil, for you are with me; your rod and your staff, they comfort me."*

That night, God wasn't a faceless being far off somewhere. I felt like he was a good father who stepped down from heaven in order to sit beside me and listen. Just like my husband holding our nine-month-old all night who has a fever and ear infection, he didn't take the pain away, he just held her. God just stayed with me.

Now I wish I could say that that night God came down and healed me. And from then on I had joy overflowing and my pregnancy was a breeze. It wasn't, but I can say that that night stands out in my mind as the night things changed for me. That was when I started on the journey that landed me here—sharing what I learned with you.

WHY WAS THIS BOOK WRITTEN FOR YOU?

My desperate cry and subsequent prayer life has impacted me in two ways, and those are the same two reasons I wrote this book. Our relationship with God should never end with us; we are invited in and then sent out to battle. You are invited into a relationship with him, and this book is how he wants to engage you.

1. **Invite:** God has given me a message for you. A message that he loves you, wants a relationship with you and can't wait to walk with you in a new and deeper way that will change your life...this relationship that has and continues to change my life is for you too! I want to share what I have learned as a way of pointing you to our father in heaven who wants me—and he wants you. I can't wait to tell you how much he loves you. As he has shown me how much he loves you, it is making me love you too!

2. **Fight:** God not only wants to be close with you and talk with you every day but he wants to go into battle with you. In our relationship with God, he wants to

show us how the skills and gifts he has given each of us are meant to battle against the darkness of this world. If you are reading this book, he wants to use you in this battle that is so much bigger than you and me. This is the battle since the beginning of time and you are way too important to be sitting on the sidelines. All you have to do is say, "Yes."

Jesus' last words to the disciples in Matthew 28:18-20 were:

> *"All authority in heaven and on earth has been given to me. Go therefore and make disciples of all nations, baptizing them in the name of the Father and of the Son and of the Holy Spirit, teaching them to observe all that I have commanded you. And behold, I am with you always, to the end of the age."*

He wants to be with us and he wants to equip and use us for the kingdom of God. That is why I am here—to deliver this message and to equip you with the greatest tool we have: prayer.

Prayer is a relationship and prayer is how we fight.

In my process of learning how to have a powerful and active spiritual walk there were three habits that when practiced regularly were so transformative. Not only did they bring me joy, inward enrichment, and peace but there are tangible blessings that affect and infect others (because this kind of joy is contagious). The three habits are:

1. Prayer
2. Study of Scripture
3. Practicing Righteousness (this includes confession of
   sin and obedience to God)

This book teaches you the basic principles of how to pray, but we will dip into the other two habits as well. Just like the analogy in Ecclesiastes 4:12 of a rope with three strands not easily being broken, these three habits working in tandem are a prime example of such a powerful rope that is strong and usable. All to say we can't discuss prayer without touching on these other two habits, so they will come up as we go along.

PRACTICE MAKES EXPERT

Just like any skill, if practiced often enough, prayer can become both a beneficial habit and useful skill. Many people attribute that Albert Einstein said, "If anyone spends 15 minutes a day learning something new, in a year, he [or she] will be an expert; in 5 years, a national expert."[1] I don't know about you, but I can give fifteen minutes a day to become a prayer expert. At the end of each principle there will be a practice opportunity that you can use to work on your prayer skills. Each practice is meant to take fifteen minutes and be practiced for a week.

INVITATION TO RELATIONSHIP

Psalm 23 is one of those texts that we've heard on repeat, but man is it powerful! David wrote it when he was desperate and on the run from Saul. This psalm is the picture God gave him to answer his cry of desperation. God didn't show him a picture of the heavenly armies coming down and killing all David's enemies. He gave him a picture of the relationship God wants with him—a relationship that is the answer to our desperation, our source of peace and a promise that our shepherd is always beside us. God's answer may not always be deliverance, but it is a relationship.

As we start this journey together, I want to take some pressure off you. I have fallen into the mental trap that I can be close to God and be used by him when I… fill in the blank. When I am less busy, when I am older, when I don't cuss anymore, when I am a more patient mom… the list goes on. But I think the picture of us as sheep in Psalm 23 is God's way of saying that he doesn't need anything from us and wants us to come as we are into a relationship with him. Sheep are stupid, defenseless, and can literally do nothing to care for themselves. I don't think this means that God thinks we are stupid, I just think he wants you to know that he isn't in love with a future version of you. God is in love with you now and wants to walk with you and be with you through every high and low. If he can love a sheep, he can love you, his beloved child, in every stage of your life and wants to be with you through it all.

I recently rewatched some home videos of when my son was learning to walk. I and his two older sisters were all cheering him on and we all three rushed to help him when he fell. I wasn't waiting around for him to figure out walking before I would be with him—I was right by his side, cheering his success and supporting him in his failures. This is the invitation of Psalm 23 and the invitation for us today. Step into a relationship with God and let him parent and shepherd you. I didn't look at my son with annoyance or judgment when he fell. I helped him up and walked beside him. That is what this book is, an invitation and a battle plan. Keep in mind this is just an overview but I do hope that just like that night when I was pregnant, this marks the start of something new for you. Something that will change your life. So I've got two questions for you:

Are you desperate?
What if you pray?

---

1. "Find 15 Minutes a Day Learning Something New. Einstein Said That If..." *Heroic,*www.heroic.us/quotes/daniel-g-amen-tana-amen/find-15-minutes-a-day-learning-something-new-einstein-said.

CHAPTER 1
PRINCIPLE ONE: THE RELATIONSHIP

I was blessed to grow up in the church. With that blessing came the gift of learning Scripture and accepting Christ at a young age. But my sinful self still found a way to corrupt that gift because I believed that my knowledge and good deeds were what saved me. Imagine me, a seven-year-old sitting on the front row of the Sunday school classroom at church with her hand up ready to answer any and every question. As a goody two-shoes trying to earn my salvation, I learned the pillars of our faith backwards and forwards:

1. We are sinners in need of a Savior.
2. God is a good God.
3. He sent His Son to die on the cross for our sins.
4. If we believe He died on the cross for our sins and accept Him into our hearts, we will spend eternity with him.

I thought I was holding my ticket to heaven with these four beliefs in my hands. I had the faith like it said in Hebrews 11:6:

> *"And without faith it is impossible to please him, for whoever would draw near to God must believe that he exists and that he rewards those who seek him."*

But then I read James 2:19:

> *"You believe that God is one; you do well. Even the demons believe—and shudder!"*

Does anyone else feel like James is mocking us here with his "you do well"? It is like he is saying in a sarcastic tone, "Oh wow, you believe that God is one? Well good for you! Even the demons, who are not saved, believe the truth of who God is!" James is arguing that mere belief won't save us. Even the demons know and believe the four truths above. In fact, they know them better than we do, and they shudder at the thought of God's power. What separates us from the demons? What ensures that when we die and knock on the door of heaven, we are let in instead of rejected?

THE DIFFERENCE

We not only need faith, but we need a loving relationship.

In Matthew 25:1–13 Jesus shares a parable (a parable is a relatable story used to teach his listeners):

> *"Then the kingdom of heaven will be like ten virgins who took their lamps and went to meet the bridegroom"* (v. 1).

This represents humankind at the end of our lives or Jesus' return. Scripture is clear that we should always be prepared for Jesus' return, for he will come like a thief in the night (Revelation 16:15). Five of the virgins were prepared; five were not. The point being that, if you are waiting to get your life together later, this is your sign that waiting won't work. We need to be prepared for Jesus' return now. And when he does come, if you aren't prepared, you get left behind. He isn't waiting for you to get your act together, he wants to get to know you today. The unwise who were not prepared not only missed the opportunity to meet the bridegroom but when they finally got to the door where the bridegroom was they were rejected. The unprepared virgins represent those who don't have a relationship with Jesus. When they knock on the door to be let in, and say, "Lord, Lord, open to us" (v. 11), he will answer, "Truly, I say to you, I do not know you" (v. 12). The point I am making is that he doesn't say, "You didn't believe," or "You didn't do enough good," but "I didn't know you." The only thing separating us from the demons is our loving relationship with him. Not our merit. Not our knowledge. Not our belief, but our relationship.

FAN GIRL

The same thing would happen to me if I knocked on Justin Timberlake's door. Now listen, I have been a JT fan for years; N'SYNC was on my playlist constantly when I was a teenager. But, it doesn't matter how many facts I know about Justin or even if I believe I love him, if I show up and knock on his door, he is not letting me in. He doesn't know me! He doesn't care how many times I've listened to his work, contributed to his bank account or told others how awesome he is. In fact, if I try to burst into his house, his bodyguard will probably stop me and lead me in the OPPOSITE direction.

In contrast, every morning my daughter wakes up, charges down the stairs to sit in her daddy's lap, and he asks her how she slept while he drinks his coffee. Her dad takes her on dates where they talk and discuss what she is learning in school, how she feels about friends, what she's excited about, and what makes her sad. So, what will happen when she knocks on our front door as an adult? Her daddy will let her in without hesitation because he is her dad. She knows him, she talks to him daily and has a relationship with him. Does she know facts about him? Yes, but she also loves to spend time with him as much as possible. I have no doubt in my mind that when she knocks on our door, he will fling the door open and grab her in a bear hug if he wasn't already waiting for her outside when she arrives. There will not be a second of doubt in her mind that she will be welcomed like family when she knocks on that door. God feels the exact same way about us when we know him personally.

When God saves us and we cry out and confess Jesus as our Savior, he doesn't just save us from a life of misery or deliver us from hell. He brings us into his family—a family with the most incredible father of all time. (See Ephesians 1:5.) God is not one of these grumpy couch potato dads who is always watching TV, yelling at the kids or giving terrible advice. Nor is he a demanding angry dad who just wants his kids to stay out of his way. He is a father who wants to spend time with you, hear about everything that is going on in your life, and bring you into the kingdom-work he is doing. He doesn't get annoyed, mislead you, run out of time for you, or mistreat you in any way. He is good and can only be good and... He. Wants. A. Relationship. With. YOU.

TO KNOW

Random weird fact about me is that I love Spanish. The only two subjects I liked in school were Bible and Spanish. In Spanish they have two words that mean "to know." *Saber* is to know facts and *conocer* is to know and have met a person. They are different. And that is what I am clarifying today—conocer—KNOWING God: sitting in his lap, talking to him every day, feeling him comfort you, having relational and intimate knowledge of him.

This is the difference between the knowledge I had growing up in church and the relationship I now have. Facts are good but a relationship is better.

Knowing facts about God did not change me; my relationship with God changed me.

This morning I encouraged my children to pray and tell God about three things that happen to them throughout the day, at which point my daughter said, "But He sees everything."

I replied, "But He wants to hear it from you." He just wants you to talk to him. When we spend time with God, we not only get to know him but we become more like him. From our relationship with God comes maturity, sanctification, and joy. Our relationship with God is the foundation that our whole Christian life is built on and the first principle that we are going to study.

JOY IN OUR RELATIONSHIP

Psalm 16:11 says,

> "In your presence there is fullness of joy; at your right hand are pleasures forevermore."

Psalm 4:7 says,

> "You have put more joy in my heart than they have when their grain and wine abound."

The relationship I am talking about is what led the psalmist to write these two verses. A relationship that brings us joy and pleasure, more than anything we can find here on earth like "food or wine." God is inviting us to be close with him and he wants our relationship with him to bring us joy. He isn't saying, be perfect and then you will have joy. But be with me.

One of my favorite pictures in our home is the picture of me holding my son for the first time. No one quite captured the moment with my two previous children like my husband did when my son was born. But when they flipped that baby up on my stomach, even though the pain of the last ten hours was still fresh—no pain that child caused me could keep me from the overwhelming joy of holding him. Not because of anything he had done or would do, but because He. Is. Mine. God wants us like this. Like a mother longing to see her baby for the first time. A mother who had suffered dearly for that child, the suffering made me love him more. God suffered for you. He loves you so much he saw you dead and sent his son to die for you to save you. You did nothing to save yourself and you did nothing to be adopted into his family.

Ephesians 2:1–2, 4, 8–9 says,

> "And you were dead in the trespasses and sins in which you once walked...But God being rich in mercy, because of the great love with which he loved us, even when we were dead in our trespasses...for by grace you have been saved through faith. And this is...not a result of works, so that no one may boast."

He didn't save you to sit you over in a corner, he saved you INTO a relationship with him. Back in Ephesians 1:4–5 Paul says,

> "In love he predestined us for adoption to himself."

BE REAL WITH GOD

Like we just saw in Ephesians 2, God knows where you come from. He is not surprised by any shortcomings or failures. An intimate relationship with God, like an earthly one, isn't showing him your prettiest face all the time. It's letting God see all of you—every version—without a filter. He wants to rejoice with you when you rejoice, and mourn when you mourn. God wants in on all of the good and bad with you. Think about your closest relationships—how do you talk to those people? What is the difference between how you speak to a close friend and how you interact with an acquaintance? In your close relationships, do you feel pressured to say certain words to impress them?

My daughter recently injured her big toe pretty badly; she was playing too rough with her siblings and fell. We thought she broke it. She had to use a boot and crutches for the next week. She was weak, crying a lot and if I'm honest not the most pleasant person to be around. What do you think her father, who she crawls up into his lap every day did? He carried her. All week he gave her piggy back rides up and down the stairs. When she was crying, when she was cranky, he was there. He didn't leave her—she was honest about her weakness, and he met her needs. He couldn't do that if she wasn't honest about her weakness.

We have to let God see all of us—to be fair, he already knows anyway.

But he wants to hear it from you. Be real with God, let him carry you when you need it.

My church when I was growing up had the poem "Foot-prints" hanging in our lobby. It's a poem about a man who has a dream where he looks back at his life and there is a path of foot-prints in the sand—sometimes with one set of footprints and sometimes with two. When he asks God about this "the Lord replied, 'My precious child, I love you and will never leave you, never, ever, during your trials and testings. When you saw only one set of footprints, It was then that I carried you."[1]

PRAYER PRINCIPLE #1: GOD WANTS A RELATIONSHIP WITH YOU

To practice this: Set aside fifteen minutes of prayer every day this week. This is your invitation to talk to God like you would a close friend. Here is the kicker: don't ask him for anything. Just share with him about your day, thank him, praise him, but don't ask for anything. Disclaimer: this is transformative!

If this practice is new for you or even if you have been praying for years. I want to encourage you to linger in prayer a little longer than you are used to. When I started training at the gym, I was pretty out of shape, so I was sore a lot. My trainer always encouraged me to take a salt bath to help with the sore-ness. My first thought was, *How could there possibly be a benefit to me stewing in a hot bath of my own filth?* (As you will see in this book, I am a tad over dramatic.) But it works! I have had to learn to sit still. Just sit and let the hot water and salt do the work. I am not good at that.

I am challenging you this week to sit still, blocking out all the other sounds, thoughts and to-do's, and soak in all the goodness of your relationship with God. Just be with him. Even if it feels like you are sitting in your own thoughts at first—sit and learn to soak him in. This practice took me from just going to God with my problems to learning to talk to him. If your earthly father didn't represent this aspect of God well for you, just know

God is longing to show you the characteristics of a good father. He also wants to pursue you and know you better than anyone else. Make time for him to do this.

As you spend time with God, remember these two truths: Matthew 6:6 says,

> *"But when you pray, go into your room and shut the door and pray to your Father who is in secret. And your Father who sees in secret will reward you."*

James 4:8 says,

> *"Draw near to God, and he will draw near to you."*

---

1. Powers, Margaret Fishback. "Poem." *Footprints: The True Story behind the Poem That Inspired Millions*, Collins, Toronto, 2012.

CHAPTER 2

PRINCIPLE TWO: KNOW YOUR BIBLE

The study of Scripture is a life-changing habit. In the introduction I shared with you the three habits of our walk with God:

1. Prayer
2. Study of Scripture
3. Practicing Righteousness (this includes confession of sin and obedience to God)

This chapter is going to link the first two habits and help us see how we can pray while we read Scripture.

TRUTH VS LIES

If we know Scripture, we know the truth and we know God's voice. God will never contradict himself. Also, when we understand the meta-narrative—the whole story of the Bible—it helps us see him clearly and be able to tell the difference between truth and lies.

When I turned sixteen, my first job was at the local bank. I was the receptionist and I sat next to the bank tellers. One day I heard them training a new teller. Part of the training is to teach the person how to see the difference between a real dollar bill and a fake. I remember thinking that they were about to pull out a fake bill to study but the training teller just said, "Here is a real hundred dollar bill." She went on to point out specific traits on the bill that can't be forged. Then she said, "If you know the real bills, you can always spot a fake." This is true of Scripture as well. If we know the Word, we can spot lies in our thoughts and beliefs, and even in the words and beliefs of others.

After Jesus was baptized by John, he "was led up by the Spirit into the wilderness" where he fasted for forty days and nights (Matthew 4:1, NKJV). Satan, knowing Jesus was hungry, challenged him to prove his sonship by turning nearby stones into bread. Jesus quotes Deuteronomy 8:3 and responds,

> "Man shall not live by bread alone, but by every word
> that proceeds from the mouth of God" (v. 4, NKJV).

Jesus used scripture to defeat Satan's lies and deception. Not only does Jesus show us how to fight deception with the truth found in the Bible, but he reminds us of our spiritual need for it. God's Word will feed us and keep us.

I was reminded of this when my family and I read the *Chronicles of Narnia* series by C.S. Lewis. In the scene from *The Lion, The Witch and The Wardrobe* where (spoiler alert) Aslan was going to be killed because of Edmund's sin, we saw a powerful example of discerning truth from lies. You see, Edmund believed a lie about the deceptive queen, acted on that belief (which was a huge mistake), and Aslan who was innocent had to take his place. At this point my kids started to scream and cry that it wasn't fair. I paused reading the book to remind them that Edmund refused to listen to the truth. Both Lucy and the wise beavers pleaded with him that the queen was evil and not to be trusted. But Edmund rejected the truth and ran to the queen instead. No matter what his sister Lucy or the beavers said, Edmund refused to listen. Edmund should have died for such treachery, but Aslan (who represents Jesus) died in his place.[1]

This is so important: knowing the Word helps us to discern the truth. We are just like Edmund—so easily distracted by all the yummy things the world has to offer. When the queen tempted him with the Turkish delight, he only thought about his stomach and didn't care about the truth. But, just like the enchanted Turkish delight, the world's delights only lead us astray. We have to know the Bible to be able to discern the truth, and that includes knowing when we are being deceived. God gave us his Word because he knows we cannot see the truth on our own. Isaiah 55:8–9 says,

> *"For my thoughts are not your thoughts, neither are your ways my ways, declares the LORD. For as the heavens are higher than the earth, so are my ways higher than your ways and my thoughts than your thoughts."*

This verse is God's way of saying, you may be smart, but sometimes you can be deceived and can't see the difference between truth and lies on your own. You need me. We need Scripture to know the truth about God, know the truth about who we are and what we are called to do.

THE THREE QUESTIONS

However, understanding Scripture isn't as clear as one may hope. It is multidimensional and complex.

Understanding and applying what God is saying takes practice.

Through much trial and error, as well as arrogance and humility, I have come up with a formula that I want to offer you. It isn't perfect but take it and make it your own. When I study the Bible, I read a passage and then discuss three questions with God:

1. God, who are you in this text?
2. God, who are you telling me I am in this text?
3. God, what are you inviting me to do because of this passage or promising me you will do?

I learned early on that I can't just read a passage and magically understand and apply it. I have to dissect, discuss and dive in. Talking with others is helpful but even more so, I needed to discuss the text with God (the author). I usually record in my journal my discussions with God so I may better understand and apply the text I've read. If we are trying to build a relationship and rapport with God, then Scripture can be a catalyst for continuing in conversation with God. When we study and internalize the truth found in Scripture about who God is, who we are, and what he calls us to do, we can avoid the traps and pitfalls of the enemy. One of the oldest tricks in Satan's repertoire is to convince us that God isn't good and shouldn't be trusted. (See Genesis 3.)

My first question for God—Who are you in this text? —is important because the world around us does not speak truth about who God is, Scripture does. We can't physically see God, but if we allow Scripture to define who he is, it paints a picture of the God who wants to have a relationship with us. Like we saw in Psalm 23 when God showed himself as the shepherd; he wants us to see that he loves us, is watching over us and will never leave us. A shepherd even sleeps with the sheep. This is who God is showing us that he is, and he does this in many different places in Scripture. This helps us to see who we are talking to when we pray.

My second question—Who are you telling me I am in this text? —is important because what God says about us is the fundamental part of our identity. When we consider God's identity and our identity (specifically how God sees us) it should impact the way we view ourselves.

The world says we are male/female, old/young, smart/stupid, pretty/ugly, successful/failure but God says, "Mine."

None of those other qualities are as important as this truth. What he says about us is who we are FIRST.

Sure, some of those other things may still be true, but like it says in Galatians 3:26–29,

> *"For in Christ Jesus you are all sons of God, through*
> *faith. For as many of you as were baptized into*
> *Christ have put on Christ. There is neither Jew nor*
> *Greek, there is neither slave nor free, there is no*
> *male and female, for you are all one in Christ Jesus.*
> *And if you are Christ's, then you are Abraham's*
> *offspring, heirs according to promise."*

When I first read this, I questioned, *Why doesn't it say you are "sons AND DAUGHTERS"*? Research revealed, at that time in history men had way more value than women. So when he just says "sons" he is inferring that in Christ we are all of equal value. Again, verse 28 says, "There is no male and female." We are beloved children of God, no matter how the world defines us. Our sonship is our first identifier. This shows us who we are but also how we are viewed—we are loved, chosen and heirs.

My third question for God is basically: "So what do I do with this information?" This is the application step where we take the truth of the text and respond to it in some way. Sometimes the text will give us specific commands or clear promises that we can apply to our lives or use as reminders of who God is and the confidence we can have in him. Not all texts in Scripture are easy to apply; for example, some of the genealogies or directions for making the temple or ark. But they are applicable when looked at as part of the whole story.

Let's use these three questions to examine a text that talks specifically about our relationship with God. My goal in doing this is to bolster our Bible study time by looking at one way that I have learned to interact with Scripture. It's a simple technique that merges the study of Scripture with talking to God. I know this is thorough but bear with me—just to see the process in action.

THE VINE AND HIS BRANCHES

John 15:1–11 is a wonderful analogy that helps us understand the ideal of what our relationship with God can look like and how it can impact our life. Take time now to read John 15:1–11 and I will walk through it with you using the three questions I previously asked.

> "11 am the true vine, and my Father is the vinedresser.
> 2 Every branch in me that does not bear fruit he
> takes away, and every branch that does bear fruit he
> prunes, that it may bear more fruit. 3 Already you

are clean because of the word that I have spoken to you. 4 Abide in me, and I in you. As the branch cannot bear fruit by itself, unless it abides in the vine, neither can you, unless you abide in me. 5 I am the vine; you are the branches. Whoever abides in me and I in him, he it is that bears much fruit, for apart from me you can do nothing. 6 If anyone does not abide in me he is thrown away like a branch and withers; and the branches are gathered, thrown into the fire, and burned. 7 If you abide in me, and my words abide in you, ask whatever you wish, and it will be done for you. 8 By this my Father is glorified, that you bear much fruit and so prove to be my disciples. 9 As the Father has loved me, so have I loved you. Abide in my love. 10 If you keep my commandments, you will abide in my love, just as I have kept my Father's commandments and abide in his love. 11 These things I have spoken to you, that my joy may be in you, and that your joy may be full."

After reading the text, what stands out to you? Generally, after I read a passage, I like to take a moment to summarize the text; even if it's just in my mind. My summary of this passage looks like this: Jesus paints a picture of a vine, a branch and a vinedresser in a vineyard.

Next, I begin to ask God the three questions:

God, who are you in this text?

Verse 1 says, "I am the true vine, and my Father is the vinedresser."

As I read and answer the question, I take note of what I know is true about the vine and vinedresser. We see two persons of God expressed in this verse. Jesus, God the Son, is narrating the story, while God the Father is the vinedresser. A vinedresser is a person who specializes in growing and tending to vines so they will produce fruit. The vinedresser oversees the process with delicate, intentional care. He watches over the soil and the weather. He does all he can to protect and ensure the plant's success, even pruning the vine's branches so it will bear more fruit. He is not too busy to care for the vine, in fact his name here indicates he is a caretaker of the vine. As I dwell on this passage, the words paint a picture in my mind of who God is. Now I move on to question number two.

God, who are you telling me I am in this text?

I see the answer in verse 5:

> "I am the vine; you are the branches. Whoever abides in
> me and I in him, he it is that bears much fruit, for
> apart from me you can do nothing."

Jesus is saying that we are the branches. This means we are dependent on and supplied by the vine. We have a very intimate relationship with the vine, and we depend on the vinedresser who cares for us. This is already such a rich picture for me where I see God the Father tending to me as the vinedresser, and Jesus wanting me to rely on him as my vine.

Also, the word "abide" is important here. Abide is an active verb meaning to remain or stay. The Hebrew-Greek Keyword Study Bible NASB edition defines "abide" in a beautiful way, saying it is "used in the absolute sense, with the idea of perpetuity. To remain or endure forever... to remain united with him."[2] This idea of permanence is important because it gives us peace.

God isn't going to leave us; he is all in.

Next, I want to know what this picture means for me today, so I ask:

God, what are you inviting me to do because of this passage or promising me you will do?

In verse 4 we see our instructions and promise:

> *"Abide in me, and I in you. As the branch cannot bear fruit by itself, unless it abides in the vine, neither can you, unless you abide in me."*

Or in other words, "commit and spend time with me and I am committed to spend time with you. You will bear fruit if you are committed to spending time with me."

Jesus, God the Son, is the true vine. In this context, *true* means the perfect and only. He is the one who bridges the gap connecting us to the soil, which has the water and nutrients we so desperately need. It is easy to focus on the branch's fruit production, but fruit cannot be produced without the actual relationship between the branch and the vine. A branch separated from a healthy vine produces no fruit! The fruit we produce is the overflow of our relationship with God; like how a loving marriage is intended to produce children. The overflow of our relationship with God is listed out in Galatians 5:22–23,

> *"But the fruit of the Spirit is love, joy, peace, patience, kindness, goodness, faithfulness, gentleness, self-control."*

He loves us so much and he wants us to produce these things. Think about what is on this list—are these things you want? Jesus promises to provide all we need if we stay connected to him. My takeaway here is that he wants me to depend on him and he WANTS to be the provider of all I need. This is an intimate relationship with God.

After reading John 15 and answering those three questions, we can see the way God wants our relationship with him to look. He wants it to be intimate, where we are daily dependent on him. He wants to know us like the vinedresser knows the vine and he wants to supply all we need through our relationship with him. How does it feel to hear that the God of the universe wants a relationship with you like this? So often in Scripture God communicates his love for us and his desire to be in relationship with us. Studying the Word and discussing the texts with him through prayer helps us get these truths in our head.

Finally, after I discuss the passage with him using the three questions above, I like to say it all back to him as a prayer:

God thank you for providing me with all I need by being not only my vine but also my vinedresser. Please remove any branch from me that does not bear fruit and help me to see the sin I commit that leads me away from you. Please help me to bear fruit. I need your help so that I can do what you have made me to do. Show me what it looks like to abide in you and remind me when I forget that you abide in me. You are my vine, and I am the branch. I cannot bear fruit on my own, I need to abide in you. Show me how. Apart from you, I can do nothing.

This is how I take the time to learn the truth, use it to prune out lies in my mind, learn God's voice and use Scripture to build my relationship with God. This took less than ten minutes and it is an example of how we will practice our second prayer principle.

———

PRAYER PRINCIPLE #2: KNOW YOUR BIBLE

To practice this: This sounds simple, but it is powerful. During your fifteen minutes with God, start your time like you did last week. Spend time talking to him like he is a friend and don't ask him for anything. Then, use these three questions to study the Lord's prayer in Matthew 6:1–15.

1. God, who are you in this text?
2. God, who are you telling me I am in this text?
3. God, what are you inviting me to do because of this passage or promising me you will do?

When we hear a passage over and over like we have this one it is easy to look past the true meaning of the text. This passage is rich and layered in the truths God wants us to know. He has a message for you about who he is, who he thinks you are and the relationship he wants to have with you. Through this prayer we see Jesus lay out a conversation he wants us to have with God the Father. I pray you see it in a whole new light as you study.

———

1. Lewis, C. S. "Fourteen, The Triumph of the Witch." *The Chronicles of Narnia*, HarperCollins Children's Books, London, 2014.
2. Zodhiates, Spiros. *Hebrew-Greek Key Word Study Bible: Key Insights into God's Word: NASB, New American Standard Bible*. AMG Publishers, 2008.

CHAPTER 3
PRINCIPLE THREE: KNOW YOUR GOD

have an older cousin. When we were kids, she thought I was the most annoying person on the planet. She always rolled her eyes when I talked, left me out of games and made fun of me. In contrast my aunt always told me I was hilarious and loved to talk to me. She would take me out for dinner, loved to introduce me to her friends and still calls me regularly. I love to talk to her. I always felt like I was on trial and had to prove myself when I was around my cousin, but I feel loved and important when I talk to my aunt. How people view us, or how we THINK they view us, affects how we talk to them. How God sees us, or how we think he sees us, affects how we relate to him. We want to talk to people who want to talk to us. And God wants to talk to us! We get to know God and how he views us in studying the Bible. Which is where we are going now. How we see God, and how we understand his view of us, affects how we engage with him. Knowing your Bible and knowing your God go together.

WHO IS GOD?

This is an important question to ask. When we know the Bible, we will know our God. Our relationships with people are physical and audible. We can see our friends, talk to them, and use all our senses to engage with them. However, engaging with God is different. Reading the Bible allows us to see and understand him. But we can't just read the Bible; we must study it and engage with it. I pray my three questions from chapter two have helped you look at the Bible in a new way. Once you have built a strong foundation of Scripture study and understanding, you can more easily address this most important question: Who is God?

Each person's unique characteristics impact how we speak to and interact with them. My aunt is kind, a good listener, an encourager and cares about me. That is why I like to talk to her. A person's qualities affect how we relate to them. The same is true about God. Who we believe he is, affects how we relate to him. Studying Scripture to understand and know God's character has made a huge impact on the way I talk to him. Let's look at a verse that has helped me a great deal.

GOD IS LOVE

I want to start with a characteristic that is a cultural favorite right now: "God is love." This statement is taken from 1 John 4:7–8:

> "Beloved, let us love one another, for love is from God,
> and whoever loves has been born of God and knows
> God. Anyone who does not love does not know God,
> because God is love."

Ok, that verse is a great start on its own. After reading that, I would think, *I kinda like this guy.* What if we take it a step further? What is love? Does Scripture define it for us? If you have ever been to a wedding, you have probably heard 1 Corinthians 13:4–7. It says that no matter how awesome or successful or smart or faithful a person is, they are nothing without love. What is love?

Love is patient.

Love is kind.

Love does not envy or boast.

Love is not arrogant or rude.

Love doesn't keep a record of wrong.

Love is not irritable or resentful.

Love does not rejoice in wrongdoing but rejoices with the truth.

Love bears all things, believes all things, hopes all things, endures all things. Love Never Fails.

If God is love, then can we exchange the word "love" for the word "God" in this passage? Here is what it would look like:

God is patient.

God is kind.

God does not envy or boast.

God is not arrogant or rude.

God doesn't keep a record of wrong.

God is not irritable or resentful.

God does not rejoice in wrongdoing but rejoices with the truth.

God bears all things, believes all things, hopes all things, endures all things. God never fails.

The scriptural truth of who God is impacts the way I want to talk to him. If he isn't irritable, then I can pray relentlessly at any hour of the day and never think I am annoying. If he doesn't keep a record of wrong, then I know he doesn't hold my past sins against me or make fun of me but truly forgives me. If he is patient, then he doesn't roll his eyes when I sin. Like a kind parent whose child is learning to walk, when I stumble, he helps me back up and keeps encouraging me until I can walk on my own. Does engaging with God as listed above change the way you feel about him? Does it change the way you feel you can talk to him? It does for me! I encourage you to pause here and pray and ask God to reveal any ways you need to view him as he is in this verse.

GOD AS FATHER

The next two characteristics of God I want to discuss we see in Matthew 6. In this passage, Jesus sets an example for how we ought to pray, or in other words how we talk to God. Before his prayer, Jesus refers to God as "your Father who is in heaven" (v. 1). Then, when he begins to pray, he starts by saying, "Our Father in heaven" (v. 9). Jesus wants us to see God as our Father. God is the perfect example of what a father should be. He cares, he listens, he is for us and loves to be with us!

Although I am an imperfect parent, I still see glimpses of God's father-ness swell up in both me and my husband with our kids. God as Father is not mirrored after earthly fathers. God is the perfect picture of what a father should be.

When I was on vacation with my family in Mexico, my five-year-old daughter slipped on a water slide and cut a deep two-inch gash in her chin. My husband doesn't speak Spanish as well as I do, so I took her to the ER. On the way, I held and comforted her, as well as tried to be silly and cheer her up because the amount of blood really scared her. When we got to the ER I paid the driver to stay and wait for us and worked with the nurses to get her checked in, all in Spanish mind you, a language my daughter doesn't speak.

Finally, the doctor decided that Liv needed stitches and wanted to put her under general anesthesia so it would be easier and quicker for him. As her parent, it was my job to think through and make the decision. I had previously researched the risks associated with anesthetizing a child under the age of ten. I remembered reading that it should only be used for a true emergency. As a five-year-old, Liv didn't know the implications of being put under anesthesia, and I felt the weight of making that decision for her. Even though I often trust and accept medical advice from professionals, I knew in this case that the risks weren't worth it. The battle with the doctor (who spoke no English) was not pleasant. He didn't want to have to deal with Liv moving, which in my mind wasn't an "emergency" or worth the risks associated with her going under anesthesia. So, I prayed, and I fought, and I won, of course because I will fight for any and everything my children need.

When we finally got Liv on the operating table, I coached her through the process. I held her while a rough and somewhat annoyed doctor put five stitches in her chin. She screamed, but because I worked with her, she didn't move. I fought with the nurses and doctor in a language I only speak moderately well. Yet, I fought to protect, encourage, and do what was best for my child.

If I, who am an imperfect parent, would do this, how much more will our perfect Father in heaven fight for us? (See Matthew 7:11, ESV.) He wants to battle for us, hold us, encourage and be with us through every step of our lives. Under no circumstance would I ever leave my children when they are in need. Why do we so often question if God will? I think he knows this about us, that we easily forget the truth about him, so Jesus tells us in Luke 11:11–13:

> "What father among you, if his son asks for a fish, will
> instead of a fish give him a serpent; or if he asks for
> an egg, will give him a scorpion? If you then, who
> are evil, know how to give good gifts to your chil-

dren, how much more will the heavenly Father give
the Holy Spirit to those who ask him!"

On top of being loving, there are so many ways that God sees
and understands the picture better than we can—just like me
with Liv, and he wants to lead us. Romans 11:33–36 reminds us
of this truth,

> *"Oh, the depth of the riches and wisdom and knowledge*
> *of God! How unsearchable are his judgments and*
> *how inscrutable his ways! 'For who has known the*
> *mind of the Lord, or who has been his counselor?'*
> *'Or who has given a gift to him that he might be*
> *repaid?' For from him and through him and to him*
> *are all things. To him be glory forever. Amen."*

There are many more scriptures about God as the Father. I
encourage you to look into them: Isaiah 64:8, 1 John 3:1, Psalm
103:13, and the list goes on. Let Scripture show you what it
means for him to be Father. Remember: we do not model our
view of God after earthly fathers. They are not perfect. God is
the perfect model. So no matter how good or bad your earthly
father was, find the truth of God as Father in Scripture.

Don't solely base your view of the God of the universe on
your experience with your earthly father.

Jesus wants to remind us that God is a loving father who is
for our good and fights for us. This is who we are talking to.

GOD AS SOVEREIGN KING

The verse, 'Our Father in heaven' is also meant to remind us that not only is God our loving Father, but He is seated on a throne in heaven. This is who we are praying to. I love the way David paints this very image of God on a throne in 1 Chronicles 29:11–13:

> *"Yours, O LORD, is the greatness and the power and the*
> *glory and the victory and the majesty, for all that is*
> *in the heavens and in the earth is yours. Yours is the*
> *kingdom, O LORD, and you are exalted as head*
> *above all. Both riches and honor come from you, and*
> *you rule over all. In your hand are power and*
> *might, and in your hand it is to make great and to*
> *give strength to all. And now we thank you, our*
> *God, and praise your glorious name."*

Our heavenly father is THE Sovereign King with all power, all knowledge and who rules over everything. This should give us confidence when we pray.

When I was a teenager I worked for my awesome aunt who was the event coordinator at Texas Lil's Dude Ranch. Lil was the owner who built the 192-acre dude ranch to its former glory. As a thirteen-year-old it was one of the coolest places I had ever been. They did huge events and parties, team building cattle drives and concerts. It had a large dance hall, outdoor pavilions, a giant slide into the river, a pool, carnival area, petting zoo and childcare area, which is where I worked. I remember one day during a big event news started traveling that Lil herself would be on the ranch that day. My aunt came to me excitedly and said, "Lacey, be on your best behavior, Lil is here." The implication being, Lil is the owner and operator, and she could fire me. Lil was one of those women who made heads turn when she entered a room: big blonde hair, cowboy hat, always in sequins and bright colors, cowboy boots to match every outfit and a huge contagious smile. All of this was amusing from far away but when I heard her heeled boots entering the kids' corral area where I worked, real fear sparked inside of me.

She walked up to me and asked, "Are you Annie's niece, Lacey?" I just stared for a moment before I remembered the answer.

"Yes. I mean, yes ma'am, that is me." Then came the sweaty palms as I waited to find out if I was in trouble. I didn't exhale until she smiled big and laughed, "My goddaughter was here last week, and she told me about you. I just wanted to tell you that you are doing a great job!"

Now, I have an awesome aunt who had trained me and praised me in this job many times; but Lil's praise meant so much more than my aunt's praise. Her authority and importance brought a healthy fear and also made her encouragement mean that much more. I can compare her authority and how it made me feel to God and how his authority as king makes us feel. He built this world and is king over it. To us, this should be a grave and weighty thought. We should fear him, but also, his words have weight and meaning because of his power and kingship. This is who we solicit when we pray. That should give us confidence that when we do make a request, he has the power to fulfill it. This belief in who he is, is called *faith*.

Psalm 147:5 says,

> *"Great is our Lord, and abundant in power; his under-standing is beyond measure."*

Part of God's authority as king is that he is All-knowing, All-powerful and Ever-present: In fancy theology talk the words are omniscient, omnipotent, and omnipresent. I remember learning these three words as a child and mispronouncing omnipotent as omni-PO-TENT and we would joke that you could also smell him everywhere. Clearly this stuck, and as a thirty-something-year-old I still chuckle. But now as I have tried to actually get to know this "smelly" God outside of the idyllic Sunday school images of my childhood; those words have more meaning. Remember, what we believe about a person affects how we speak to them. How does God's omniscience—the fact that he is all-knowing—impact how you pray to him? How about the fact that he is all-powerful and everywhere at once? This level of sovereignty is the highest of its kind. He is more sovereign than any king, ruler, or leader on earth.

CONFIDENCE IN PRAYER

So, if our Father God is good, loving, and gracious as well as all-powerful, all-knowing and ever-present, then when we pray to him, we are talking to someone who knows better than we do and cares more for us than we do.

This is who you are in a relationship with. This is who you are talking to. This is where our confidence in prayer comes from. Not only do we have confidence that we will be received like a father receives a child but confidence that whatever we ask, he has the power to do. We should shudder like the demons do at the truth of who he is like we saw in James, but also crawl into his lap like a child does their father.

If I can stack our prayer principles so far for you:

1. God Wants a Relationship with You
2. Know Your Bible
3. Know Your God

When you study and learn the Bible, you can speak to God and "conocer" or know your God.

———

PRAYER PRINCIPLES #2 AND #3: KNOW YOUR BIBLE, KNOW YOUR GOD

To practice this: During your time with God, start your time like you did the last two weeks. Spend time talking to him like he is a friend, and don't ask him for anything. Then, let's practice using Scripture to know God by looking at Psalm 23. As you read the text, answer the three questions from last week:

1. God, who are you in this text? (Remember that the God of this passage is the same God who wants to be with you today.)
2. God, who are you telling me I am in this text?
3. God, what are you inviting me to do because of this passage or promising me you will do?

Then imagine God walking with you through your day as he does in this text. Where is he when things are hard? Where is he when you don't know where to go or what to do next? Write a short paragraph to yourself describing how the God of Psalm 23 will be with you today.

CHAPTER 4

PRINCIPLE FOUR: LISTENING IN THE SILENCE

recently restarted making sourdough bread. I say restarted because I quit twice before. Making sourdough takes two skills that I don't have: the ability to follow rules and patience. If I can't sit in a salt bath for twenty minutes to soothe my aching muscles like I mentioned in chapter one, I certainly can't wait 4–8 hours for bread to rise. So both times before, after baking stale bricks for weeks instead of airy delicious bread, my sourdough experience ended in a hysterical fit of angry shouts and trashed baking materials. "Never again!" I swore to my husband. So this time when I asked my friend Malia for some sourdough starter, my husband's eyes grew to the size of baseballs and he yelled, "Not sourdough!" But this time, I did something different. I had Malia teach me and walk me through the whole process, and this time, I was patient, listened and followed directions.

The annoying thing about using sourdough starter (the rising agent that makes the bread airy and fluffy) is that it needs time. Then, on top of time, the dough needs to be mixed, kneaded and baked according to a very specific and unyielding schedule. So, thanks to Malia, my nine-year-old Elle's ability to follow directions, and three weeks of practice, I can now make delicious bread. It looks like a loaf at a bakery, and it is mouth-watering. My family of five tears through a loaf in less than 24 hours. Now I know the process, I still follow the directions to a T and finally get the results I was trying for before. A delicious homemade sourdough bread with all organic ingredients.

So why am I totally geeking out about sourdough in a book about prayer? For prayer to have its full benefit in our lives, we need patience and a little direction. When we commit to consistently sit with God in prayer, only time will show us the results we need. So being patient and willing to learn from others is a huge teacher. In this chapter, sitting patiently in silence is what I'm challenging us to do. The Bible gives us the directions, we just have to follow them and be consistent and patient.

ELIJAH AND HIS FIT

In 1 Kings 19:9–18 we see a really cool story where God comes down to speak to Elijah. I think it is interesting to point out that Elijah was in the middle of a little bit of a fit. Time and time again, God had used Elijah to defeat the enemies of Israel and as a voice piece of justice and truth. Elijah had seen God do incredible things. (See 1 Kings 18 for the last epic tale.) Yet when Jezebel, a neighboring queen, threatened Elijah, Elijah huffed off, threw himself on the ground and asked God to kill him, saying in verse 4, "It is enough; now, O Lord, take away my life, for I am no better than my fathers." As a fit-thrower myself, these stories are helpful to know what God does when we are angry and kicking our feet. God fed Elijah food and water (maybe Elijah struggled with low-blood sugar too!) and then invited him on a journey up a mountain where God would meet him. God told him to go out and stand on the mountain before the Lord. First a great wind tore at the rocks, then an earthquake shook the mountain and finally a fire sparked but God was not in the wind, the earthquake, or the fire. The text says after the fire, came "a low whisper" (1 Kings 19:12). The Hebrew for this is actually "in the silence."[1] So, Elijah heard God's voice in the silence.

I think we are similar to Elijah in that when we think of the powerful God of the universe speaking, we expect a loud God. We envision God on a stage with a booming voice, much like the Jews expected of the Messiah when Jesus came. They wanted Messiah to ride in on a powerful horse and overthrow Rome with military force but (dramatic exhale) he didn't. He came in meekness and compassion.

Jesus upsets our expectations in the best of ways. He went to the poor and the hurting, and he died a lowly death.

So what do we do with this? I say we start by getting quiet and creating a space to hear God without distraction. The world is yelling at us, but God is whispering. Go to a quiet place to hear him.

CREATING A HABIT OF PRAYER

I mentioned in the introduction, when I started my journey, I read a lot of books on prayer. One of my favorites was *Prayer: Experiencing Awe and Intimacy with God* by Timothy Keller. In chapter one he uses a powerful illustration of his wife that helped propel him into the discipline of regular prayer:

"Imagine you were diagnosed with such a lethal condition that the doctor told you that you would die within hours unless you took a particular medicine—a pill every night before going to sleep. Imagine that you were told that you could never miss it or you would die. Would you forget? Would you not get around to it some nights? No—it would be so crucial that you wouldn't forget, you would never miss."

Keller then goes on to clarify the correlation: "We have to pray, we can't let it just slip our mind."[2]

This analogy impacted him tremendously and it had the same effect on me. I remembered it six years after reading the book. There are two parts of this habit for me: the practice of having faith that prayer is that powerful, and the intimacy of regularly meeting with God. Clearing away all distraction and sitting in the quiet, talking to and listening to God is the habit I am challenging us with. Don't make him yell louder than the noises around you—put away all distraction and intentionally listen.

LISTENING TO THE ONE WHO KNOWS

My dad is a car guy. And when I say that I don't mean that he just likes cars. My dad can take a car completely apart and put it back together. When I was fifteen, I picked out a totaled car from a junkyard and my dad rebuilt it for me. It was a 1996 BMW and I thought it was the coolest thing in the whole world. It had been in an accident and the entire front half was crushed. The frame and body had to be straightened, the front end and multiple miscellaneous parts had to be replaced, and the car had to be painted. You get the idea. My dad did all of it for me. It was the best car a sixteen-year-old has ever gotten in the history of the world. I drove that thing with pride for the next ten years. One night when I was in college I went to a friend's house. Around 11pm I went to leave, but my car wouldn't start. So, who did I call? The guy who built it! I called my dad and—no joke—he asked me a few questions and figured out exactly what was wrong. He then walked me step-by-step through fixing it. Mind you, I had never taken a steering column apart before. He told me what to do and I listened to every step—it would have been foolish of me not to! My dad is the expert; I am not. I listened, followed the instructions of my father, and fixed the steering column. Within the hour I was able to drive away in a fully functioning car.

God built the world, and intentionally knit together not only you but those around you (see Psalm 139).

He has a pretty good grasp on what is going on and how to not only diagnose the issue but fix it. He is also just a prayer away and, like my dad, he will gladly sit on the call with you as long as you need. God knows everything and will gladly walk through any issue you are having at any time of day or night.

LISTENING TO GOD

Once we know God's character and voice from Scripture, we can learn how to listen for him. First, go to a quiet place where all other voices are silent. Second, pray and ask him to speak. There are two main reasons why we practice listening to God:

1. Listening to God shows God you love him and value him.
2. Listening to God is acknowledging that he is the King of kings and knows what is going on around you better than you do.

Undoubtedly, we get great direction and instruction from the Bible, but the Bible also says God can speak to us. In my experience, God has spoken to me when I sit in quiet and pray. The more I practice, the better I am at recognizing his voice.

In John 10 Jesus is telling a story about a shepherd and his sheep. He says,

> *"The sheep hear his voice, and he calls his own sheep by*
> *name and leads them out. When he has brought out*
> *all his own, he goes before them, and the sheep*
> *follow him, for they know his voice. A stranger they*
> *will not follow, but they will flee from him, for they*
> *do not know the voice of strangers" (vv. 3–5).*

PRACTICE LISTENING

When I sit quietly in prayer, I like to acknowledge that God is already aware of everything going on around me today and already has a plan for those with whom I am going to interact. I lay down my own selfish agenda and I ask him to include me in the agenda he has for those around me today and ask him to speak to me. Keep in mind, he won't say anything contrary to his character or contrary to Scripture. After this prayer, there are a few different ways that I will hear from God. Sometimes a verse will pop into my head, sometimes an encouraging word or phrase, sometimes I will see a picture or think about a friend. Then I write down the verse, thought, feeling or image and try to understand it. That is it; that is listening. Sit with God in silence and see if he will do the same thing for you.

———

BIBLICAL PRINCIPLE #4: LISTENING IN THE SILENCE

To practice this: As someone who has lived in N.Y.C. on one of the loudest streets in the U.S., I am the first to vent about how hard it is to find quiet. The street I lived on is literally referred to as "Live on Lenox." It's always loud and awake. On the other hand, I have set aside time for "quiet" and have promptly fallen asleep with my Bible in hand because I was so tired. All to say, there is grace if this one is hard for you to find. Finding quiet may not be easy but it should be intentional.

Plan to set aside quiet time for five minutes five times this week. Put away your phone, don't listen to music—be alone with your thoughts with no outside distractions. I do this in two ways. I go into my bedroom and close the door when I know my kids won't come in or I go on a walk without my phone. Spend time using some of the practices we've worked on in previous chapters and then ask God, "Is there anything you want to say to me?" If your mind wanders, have a notepad to write things down to come back to later, but really try to clear your mind and just focus on him. And remember God will not say anything that is contrary to Scripture; he will speak biblically aligned truth. Take note of anything that comes to mind: a verse, thought, feeling or image. Then ask God to explain it and see if it makes any sense. It may not be clear at first but keep trying! This is the habit that brings me so much enjoyment of God. Practice, practice, practice!

---

1. *Logos Bible Study Platform*, www.logos.com/. Accessed 1 Sept. 2023.
2. Keller, Timothy. *The Prodigal God: Recovering the Heart of the Christian Faith.* Penguin, 2008.

CHAPTER 5
PRINCIPLE FIVE: THE POSTURE OF HUMILITY AND SUBMISSION

The first four chapters were our invitation from God into a deeper relationship with him. He invites us into a relationship, invites us to get to know him through his word and to listen in the silence. This chapter starts us on the ways we can battle against our flesh and enemies around us. The first way we fight is contrary to how we might think—we start with humility and submission. I should probably preface this chapter by saying that this is a topic I avoided for a long time. I think the enemy knows how powerful humility and submission are and so he has done all he can to corrupt these two things so we misunderstand and avoid them. Let's look at a few scriptures and their promises when we humble ourselves and submit.

IF MY PEOPLE PRAY

> *If my people who are called by my name humble them-*
> *selves, and pray and seek my face and turn from*
> *their wicked ways, then I will hear from heaven and*
> *will forgive their sin and heal their land. (2 Chroni-*
> *cles 7:14).*

This verse has quite a few important commands and promises. In this chapter we will briefly skim the surface of the ideology of prayer, as given in this text. First it is important to touch on the historical context of this verse. God had pursued, chosen, blessed, rescued, fought for and protected the Israelites. By 2 Chronicles they had entered a season of peace with the reign of King Solomon. Finally they were able to build a temple for God. This verse starts with a key phrase: "My people who are called by my name." The word "people" in this verse signifies people who are saved. This is important to note because it assumes that Christians who are saved are going to need to humble themselves, pray, seek God's face, and turn from their wicked ways. Second, I want to remind us that our relationship with God is not transactional but just like any relationship there is structure that helps that relationship thrive—this is not a perfect formula, it is a beautiful invitation. So what is the actual If/Then clause in this verse? Using myself as an example, it looks like this:

If Lacey:

Humbles herself
Prays
Seeks God's face
Turns from her wicked ways

Then God will:

From heaven, hear Lacey's prayers
Forgive Lacey's sins
Heal Lacey's land

If God is a Promise Keeper—and he can only be a promise keeper (see 2 Corinthians 1:20)—then we can bank on this verse. So what do the steps look like practically? If we want to hear from God, have our sins forgiven and our land healed then we need to humble ourselves, pray, seek God, and turn from our wicked ways. Let's look a little deeper at our to-do list.

HUMBLE YOURSELF

I didn't choose humility; it is one of those things that happened to me. When I was thirteen, like most teenagers I believed the world revolved around me. I thought people were always watching me and judging me as either awesome or horrible. At all times I had to work to curate my image to show people the me I wanted them to see—this is self-obsession and pride. ME. Me. Me. One day, a strange coincidence sent a shock through my purview. During lunch, when the cafeteria was full of high school students, I walked up to the stage area where the food was served and, on my way back, in front of everyone, I did the most Kramer-esq, Three Stooges fall. It was one of those falls where you go up first—whole body horizontal and high in the air—and then slow-motion land on your back. The physical shock was nothing compared to the life-altering humility that hit me. You might think it was because everyone pointed and laughed, then I realized I could still be happy even if everyone laughed at me. Nope. In fact it was the exact opposite. Out of four hundred people, one person saw me. I sat up, looked around in shock and just stood up and walked away. You see, like me, every other teenager was focused just on themselves. This was the start of me learning humility. It was the first time I realized I wasn't the center of the universe. To my surprise, that realization was a relief. It was so freeing to know that I didn't have to be perfect at all times. It was a taste of humility.

Humility isn't something you can easily just do; humility is a state of the heart.

Humility isn't thinking less of yourself but *thinking of yourself less*. It is having a "right view" of yourself, and it is the opposite of pride. You see, pride is thinking about yourself waaaaayyyy too much—just like I did. Pride does one of two things: makes us feel like we are awesome or makes us feel like we are dirt. That is pride; the wrong view of self and thinking about yourself way too much. Unfortunately, this is the natural state of the human mind. It is thinking about me, my needs, my wants and how I feel. I have practiced this habit of pride for more of my life than I care to admit and if I am honest, doing this made me miserable. Pride made me feel like I was on a constant roller coaster going up and down from "I'm awesome" to "I'm horrible." The cure for this misery was learning about humility. Proverbs 11:2 says,

> *"When pride comes, then comes disgrace, but with the humble is wisdom."*

Solomon takes it even further—not only does pride lead to disgrace but it is sin, and God hates it. In Proverbs 8:13 he says,

> *"The fear of the LORD is hatred of evil. Pride and arro-*

gance and the way of evil and perverted speech I hate."

Then in James 4:6 it says,

"God opposes the proud but gives grace to the humble."

I don't know about you but if there is one being that I don't want against me, it is the God of the universe. And secondly, as a big ol' sinner—I need all the grace I can get. After the instance in high school, I started a quest to learn about humility and the blessing it comes with.

Learning more about humility helped me to realign with the truth of Scripture and to understand who I am in Christ. It helped to ground me on a solid biblical foundation and stop the emotional roller coaster of my pride. Humility for me was setting aside all the great and horrible things about myself and going to Scripture to see who I am. I am a sinner, daily in need of a Savior. I am an adopted child of God. Those things don't change and aren't dependent on me. Humility is the right view of self, as someone in need. Submission is yielding to a superior power. I cannot save myself so I go daily to the only one who can save me. My value in society is not about what I do or how I look, but who I am. I am a loved child of God who has been forgiven.

Why is humility important in prayer? What is the benefit? When we go to God in prayer we stop thinking about ourselves and think about God. In our prayers we are thanking and praising Him, which brings us a joyful balance of humility. Remember, Jesus taught us to pray, "Your kingdom come" (Matthew 6:10). Not my kingdom, but God's kingdom. Humility is a powerful place to start.

BIBLICAL SUBMISSION

There are two parts to humbling ourselves: humility and biblical submission. Humility is the state of the heart, submission is the fruit of humility through action. One can be submissive without humility, but true humility produces the fruit of biblical submission.

Before I jump into the topic of submission, I want to start by saying there is no perfect authority here on earth. Throughout history and certainly today there are plenty of imperfect authorities. God is the only perfect authority and the only submission I want to challenge you with here. I don't know your relationships. Please know that even though I use examples of earthly submission, I am not encouraging you to submit to anyone who mistreats or misuses you. Worldly leaders will have to give an account for their actions. Hebrews 13:17 says,

> "Obey your leaders and submit to them, for they are
> keeping watch over your souls, as those who will
> have to give an account. Let them do this with joy
> and not with groaning, for that would be of no
> advantage to you."

So now, let's talk about the benefits of submitting to a perfect God.

God is our perfect, loving, all-powerful father. He will never mistreat or misuse us. For the longest time submission was a very negative word to me because of my misunderstanding of what God was calling me to do as a woman. I thought submission meant that I had to blindly obey and follow whoever it was that was in authority over me. But when I studied the Bible to see what it actually said and then prayed and asked God to show me what the word meant, I discovered that biblical submission is stepping under the protection of a God-given authority, in this case God himself. Submission to him is for our good. We want to stand under the protection of the sovereign God of the universe. He knows everything and can protect us better than we can protect ourselves.

When I was about ten years old, I fell off the jungle bars directly onto my head. After weeks of headaches and other neck and back pain, my parents took me to a chiropractor. For the next ten plus years I saw a chiropractor weekly. Every single time he put his hands on my neck to adjust me he would say, "Don't help me. Relax and let me do it." This is submission. I could not fix my neck on my own and if I "helped" it would actually prevent him from adjusting me in order to correct my neck alignment. I had to relax my neck so he could do all the work, otherwise I stopped the healing.

This resembles the type of biblical submission we need in our spiritual walk. We need to submit to God to get the full benefit of our relationship with him. In James 4:7–8 there is a great link between submission and freedom and peace. After the verse I gave above on God opposing the proud, it says

> *"Submit yourself therefore to God. Resist the devil, and he will flee from you. Draw near to God, and he will draw near to you."*

In verse 10 it says,

> *"Humble yourselves before the Lord, and he will exalt you."*

Submission to God is how we escape slavery to sin. Then James goes on to link submission, relationship (God and I drawing close to one another), and humility.

Submission, relationship, humility—these three together give us freedom, peace, and nearness to God. This is a theme in many stories of the Old Testament as well. We saw the full effect of pride in the stories of Eve, Cain, the Tower of Babel, people during Noah's time, Pharaoh, Hebrew people (when they built a golden calf and all the 4,000 times they didn't obey and did what they wanted), Samson, Saul, over half the kings of Israel, Job's friends, and again the Hebrew people during the times of the prophets.

God celebrated and used the humility and submission of Abel, Noah, Abram, Joseph (he had to be taught it by circumstances), Moses, Joshua, Samson (at the end of his life), Deborah, Ruth, Samuel, David, Job, and then all the major and minor prophets who listened to God and spoke truth to his people. Then the ultimate and perfect picture of submission and humility is when our perfect Messiah crawled up on a cross.

Beautiful and powerful fruit comes from walking in biblical humility and submission—THAT IS WHO GOD USES.

PRACTICAL HUMILITY

One way I practice spiritual humility is by kneeling and telling God I need him to fill me up every morning. The physical act of kneeling is a sign of submitting to the power or position of the person to whom you are kneeling. We are submitting to the sovereign God of the universe, and this is not a natural state or comfortable position for us. When we kneel, it is acknowledgement of our weakness and need for God's covering, direction, and help.

I like to kneel when I pray because it puts me in the "correct" position before God. He is up in heaven on his throne, and I am down here serving him. Starting the day like this is a reminder to me to rely on him all day long. I will do it throughout the day as well, and even if I can't kneel, I will just tell God, "I need you." I humble myself by kneeling because I know the source to whom I am praying—the King over all kings. I submit to God's will when I kneel and open my hands, thanking him and praising him for all he has done, who he is, and for inviting me into a relationship with him.

How is this part of fighting? When we humble ourselves and submit to God, we are protected from sin (see James 4:8). God will not lead us astray. When we submit to him as our shepherd we are watched over and invited into a relationship with a good God (John 10:11–16). Our hearts are deceitful; we can't trust them (see Jeremiah 17:9). We are far too easily swayed by the deceitful things of the world that lead us astray (see Hebrews 13:9 and Isaiah 53:6). When we lay down our own desires and direction, we will follow a God who wants the best for us and will only ever be good to us (see Romans 8:28) and we will find joy.

––––––

PRAYER PRINCIPLE #5: THE POSTURE OF HUMILITY AND SUBMISSION

To practice this: Start your daily 5-10 minutes with God this week by kneeling (if physically able) and telling God, "I need you." Then spend some time reading over these texts to define humility: 1 Peter 5:6; Mark 9:35; Micah 6:8; Psalm 25:8–9. Now, answer the following questions:

1. Why does it say that it is GOOD for us to submit to God?
2. What is the benefit of our submission to him?
3. Ask God: What areas of my life am I submitting to you? What areas am I not?

CHAPTER 6

PRINCIPLE SIX: CONFESS AND FORGIVE

There is an old wives' tale about a woman who had a pet snake. The snake slept with her every night, usually at the foot of her bed. She loved the snake and was worried when it started having some peculiar symptoms. He stopped eating, shed his skin and started sleeping right beside her, along her side from head to toe. In her concern, she took her beloved pet to the veterinarian. After sharing the symptoms, the vet responded quickly, "You have to get rid of the snake immediately!"

The woman was saddened, "No!" she proclaimed, "I love him!"

The vet looked her dead in the eyes with a serious demeanor and said, "He is preparing to eat you."

This is the analogy we use in our house to talk about sin. You see no matter how fun sin is, how much you enjoy it and want to continue to do it—it always has one goal: to kill you. Satan uses sin to separate us from God and lead us into a prison cell of our own creation. God's laws and rules in Scripture are the same as the vet reminding us of the "pets" we are keeping that will kill us if we don't get rid of them. We are going to look at a few texts in this chapter to remind us of just that: confessing and getting rid of the sin in our lives leads us to life and peace; sin leads to death.

WHAT IS SIN?

Before we discuss confession, it's important to have a clear understanding of sin. In ancient archery "to sin" meant "to miss the mark." In Genesis 3 a perfect relationship with God was ruined by a single decision made by Adam and Eve. The serpent gave them one single choice: trust God and submit to His rules or don't trust God and do whatever you want. Adam and Eve committed the first sin when they doubted God and did whatever they wanted. Therefore, today in my life, I sin when I do two things: 1. Doubt God and 2. Do whatever I want. That is it. That is sin.

When Adam and Eve doubted God, they rejected the truth of who He is—a good and loving father—and then acted on that belief. In other words, step one of sin is believing a lie about who God is. Step two is making a decision based on that lie; and then step three is death, in case you were wondering (see James 1:15). Look at Genesis 3 and tell me that isn't exactly what Adam and Eve did! God is the all-powerful, all-knowing, loving creator of everything. Yet they trusted a small, not-all-powerful, not-all-knowing, lying, creepy snake. You see, sin isn't just breaking the rules; it is doubting the God who made the rules. And just like the snake from the beginning of the chapter—this snake isn't your friend or companion—he wants you to think he is so that he can kill you.

PARKING LOTS

Parenting has given me loads of understanding on this concept. Much like our loving Father, I have given my children rules because I love them and want them to stay alive. I remind them of this all the time by saying, "Rules are for your good" or "I'm trying to keep you alive. Will you help me?" One such rule is the protocol for walking through a parking lot. The rule is that you put a hand on Mommy, and you stay right by me until we get to the car.

A few years ago, when I had a three-year-old, two-year-old, and nine-month-old, my husband was out of town for work. This was before Uber-eats, mind you, so I had to go get dinner myself if I didn't want to cook. There was a Wingstop near my house on a busy road and the parking lot was not safe. I had practiced parking lot protocol before with my children, and we had no issues entering the building. However, on the way out, I had my nine-month-old son in one arm, my wings on the other arm, and my daughters obediently had their hands on me (part of our protocol)...at first. Suddenly my three-year-old yelled, "We don't have to obey!" and ran to my right, at which point my two-year-old followed suit and ran to my left. Keep in mind, I have no free hands so all I can do is walk into the street to stop the oncoming traffic with my body while my daughters took their lives in their own hands. My anger was real that day, and so were the consequences once I finally got them safely to the car. This is what we do when we sin and it's exactly what my kids thought, "Mommy, your rule is stupid. You don't want me to have fun. I know better, and I am going to do whatever I want."

This is sin.

TURN FROM YOUR WICKED WAYS

In the last chapter we studied 2 Chronicles 7:14 which says,

> *"If my people who are called by my name humble them-*
> *selves, and pray and seek my face and turn from*
> *their wicked ways, then I will hear from heaven and*
> *will forgive their sin and heal their land."*

The part I want to look at now is: what does it look like to "turn from your wicked ways"? It means to stop and confess your sin.

I grew up in a Christian home and was taught about Jesus as a young child. I attended church and learned the importance of obeying God's rules and avoiding "sin." I practiced these things to the best of my ability and even felt like I was doing pretty well by the time I turned eighteen. I was FCA president, a leader in my youth group, and knew my Bible back to front. One summer, I went to a teen leadership conference and the preacher started by telling us that he was going to give us a list of how to be a successful Christian leader. This is when I leaned forward to listen. The first few things on his list were helpful, then in his last point he talked about the importance of confessing sin. This is the point when I tuned that preacher out...clearly, I thought this isn't something I feel like I need to learn about. Did you not just read my list of accolades? My ways were not all that wicked. I was not a murderer, I didn't sleep around, or drink too much or break the law, so, did I really need to be taught confession? Didn't I do all the "confessing" I needed to do when I got saved? In my arrogance, I didn't listen to that teaching nor did I know there were two types of confession: confessing Jesus as Lord and Savior and confession of daily sins.

It wasn't until four years later when something was off in my life because of how miserable I felt that I finally turned my attention to the importance of confession in Scripture. I graduated from college and had to move home for the summer because a job opportunity I wanted didn't pan out. I did the only Bible study available that summer at my church. It was called Steps. During this study you take "inventory" and confess in order to experience freedom. This is when I first truly understood the verse in Matthew 5:21–22. Jesus said,

> *"You have heard that it was said to those of old, 'You shall not murder; and whoever murders will be liable to judgment.' But I say to you that everyone who is angry with his brother will be liable to judgment."*

Welp, there went my theory that I am better than a murderer!

During the process I had to confess my sins to a "mentor" that I didn't know. This was still absolutely mortifying to me even though I wasn't a "bad" sinner. I had to confess anger, fear, and pride. The first time I met with my mentor I remember sitting outside in the car terrified. I thought, I cannot go in there and tell her every horrible thing in my head. But there was a promise of freedom and joy, which is what pushed me to get out of the car. And, at the end of that meeting, that is exactly what I got!

After the lightest and slowest knock on the door (if she didn't answer I could say I tried), I walked into Kim's house and was welcomed with the cool air of peace—as if her home had the very thing I was after, the promised peace and freedom of confession. Although I could feel it surrounding me, the peace had yet to enter my core because I still held tight to the secret sins in my heart. As I sat down on her overstuffed white couch, the cool material shocked me back into the reality I was in, so my planning started: *If I confess to anger, all I have to do is say I am angry and then I can explain what the offender did, then Kim won't think I am bad, she will see I am justified in my hatred,* I thought. So after we prayed, she asked me to share a little about myself and then we started the inventory. My plan was simple: step one was to confess without any details and step two was to blame. That lasted about five minutes before Kim stopped me and said, "Lacey, I am sure you were hurt by so and so but for this process to work we need to focus on you. Our goal is to confess the sin on your side of the street, not spend all our time talking about the sins of others." *Dang it,* I thought, *but that messes up my plan!* So, I bit my tongue, and then continued: "I'm angry at my brother," (I don't have a brother, but this is an example of what I did). I started and ended abruptly. "Awesome," she said, "now let's pray this prayer:

> *Dear God, I confess my anger against John and ask for your forgiveness. John, like me, is not exempt from the fall and like me is a sinner who is forgiven by grace. Please heal my hurt, help me to forgive and bless John with peace, joy and closeness with You."*

As I repeated Kim's prayer those words worked like a skilled surgeon's hands removing the broken parts of my mind and putting my views of my brother back together whole and new. He is fallen just like me, he deserves the grace that I am seeking. He is on a journey just like I am, and I forgive him.

It was like someone opened a backpack I was carrying filled with rocks and removed them one at a time. After this first prayer, I became bolder and bolder about the sins—no longer feeling a need to blame or excuse but actually wanting to clean out that metaphorical backpack. After anger we went on to jealousy, pride, fear and shame. All the things I went in there terrified to say out loud—I boldly confessed every one. And every time, Kim didn't respond with laughter or judgment but with a prayer and a question: "Do you accept God's forgiveness?" And you know what? I did.

I left that meeting not feeling shame and embarrassment like I thought I would, but FREEDOM. I felt like I took off that heavy backpack. Through that experience, you know what I learned? Even though I am saved (and had done the first confession mentioned above), I need to confess my sins every single day. The weight of unconfessed sin isn't worth it.

It was humbling to realize that for years I had totally made God a liar because I believed I hadn't sinned and that I had nothing to confess. In 1 John 1:8–10 it says,

> *"If we say we have no sin, we deceive ourselves, and the truth is not in us. If we confess our sins, he is faithful and just to forgive us our sins and to cleanse us from all unrighteousness. If we say we have not sinned, we make him a liar, and his word is not in us."*

In God's faithfulness, He used Scripture to show me that there is freedom and joy in the confession of sin. Not shame. You see, every day for the rest of our lives we will sin and be sinned against. So, every day for the rest of our lives we need to confess our sin and forgive others. Every. Day.

When I say sin, what sin in your own life do you think of? There are two types of sin: external sins like murder, stealing, lying, adultery or the hurting of others; and there are internal sins like lust, anger, fear, hatred, etc. Both are sinning against God. I would challenge you to look at Scripture to define sin for yourself and confront your own heart daily. What sins are you giving power to in your own life?

SO THEN, WHAT IS CONFESSION?

Confession is telling God doubts you have about Him.
Confession is telling God lies you have believed about
His character.
Confession is telling God when you break the rules He
lays out in Scripture.

The main thing I want you to take away from this is that sin is a relationship blocker. Isaiah 59:2–3 says,

> *"Your iniquities have made a separation between you
> and your God, and your sins have hidden his face
> from you so that he does not hear."*

If sin causes a separation between us and God, then what brings us back into relationship with Him? Confession!

Confession of sin and forgiveness of others need to happen
in our private prayer time with God so we can continue to
be closely connected to Him.

My son gave me the opportunity to teach this to him today. I saw him hiding under a table eating something, so I bent down to see what he had.

I said, "Hey Buddy, whatcha doing?"

He said, "Nothing."

Obviously, a lie, but I kept going. "What do you have?"

With a growing look of guilt, he again said, "Nothing."

Then I did the mom look and asked, "Buddy do you want to try again? What do you think you should do right now?"

He looked guilty but also now confused. I don't think he knew what to do when he got caught in sin. I told him I would help him out. This is what I told him, and hopefully it will help you out too: When we do something wrong, our shame tells us to go and hide just like Adam and Eve did in the garden. When you feel like you need to hide from God, or in my son's case, Mommy, that is a sign that what you are doing is sin. When we hide it is like going into a jail cell and closing the door. When we accepted Christ as our Savior, we were set free. The only way we can go back to jail is by hiding in our sin, but when we confess our sin, we are again set free.

Sin puts us in prison. Confession is walking out the door.

I walked my son through confessing his sin. I said, repeat after me, "Mommy, I lied. In my cup I put ice and a full cup of sugar and was hiding from you and eating it under the table." After he repeated after me, I then asked, "How do you feel?" He responded with a smile, a hug and we did the back and forth I do with all my kids when they sin. I say repeat after me:

"Even when I sin, Mommy loves me. Even when I sin, Daddy loves me. Even when I sin, God loves me."

After we sin, we still have to accept God's forgiveness. Sometimes we also need to remind ourselves of the truth of who we are: forgiven and loved. In chapter three, we discussed who God is. Now let's look at who you (and I) are: You are a sinner that God says is to die for. You are a loved child of God who every day can run to your dad and confess your sin; and every day He will hug you, forgive you and say, "Even when I sin, Father God loves me."

FORGIVENESS

Forgiveness is a command in Scripture. In Matthew 6:14–15 we read:

> *"For if you forgive others their trespasses, your heav-*
> *enly Father will also forgive you, but if you do not*
> *forgive others their trespasses, neither will your*
> *Father forgive your trespasses."*

Even with the scary consequences in this verse, forgiveness is hard for me. I would love to say it is because of my innate sense of justice or that I am zealous for God, but my reasoning is totally sinful. I want people to pay for hurting me. I don't want to let God handle it. I want revenge.

Now before you shut this book because I am clearly a giant sinner, I will confess: my view of being sinned against is wrong and it leaves me miserable. As they say, "Unforgiveness is like drinking poison and expecting the other person to die." This is so true, unforgiveness doesn't hurt them, it hurts you. When we are sinned against it hurts, and sometimes we believe the lie that forgiving someone means that we are saying what they did wasn't wrong, but it doesn't mean that. God takes sin seriously and He is very protective of His children. He hates when we are hurt, but His view of us does not change. Our identity also does not change when we are sinned against.

Forgiveness is releasing the ledger of the offense against us and saying in our hearts, "You owe me nothing."

The offender is released from the debt they owe you. Jesus'

parable in Matthew 18:21–28 is a helpful example of this. Unforgiveness is like grabbing someone by the shirt and saying, "Pay me what you owe!" like the unforgiving servant says in verse 28. Forgiveness is what the master does in verse 27: "The master of that servant released him and forgave him the debt."

A note to those who have had a horrible offense done to them: what happened to you was not okay. I am in no way asking you to condone any sin done against you. I only want to make sure you are not allowing past offenses to continue to hold you captive. If you let offense have its way, it can change your identity and what you believe about yourself. Don't. I've heard abuse victims say that unforgiveness felt like the abuse kept happening to them over and over until they were finally able to forgive, and then it was like the cycle stopped. The abuse was not your fault, God hates what happened to you and He wants to heal you! Let Him! Trust Him to be your advocate and take vengeance on your behalf. (See Romans 12:19.)

We live in a fallen world and every single person on this planet is a sinner—and that is true in the church as well. Every day for the rest of your life you are going to be sinned against. You can drink the poison of unforgiveness, or you can let God work through the hurt to make you more like Christ and forgive. It is your choice. But when you feel like the sin against you is too great to forgive, ask God for help. I prayed for years for help forgiving someone who hurt me. It took daily prayer and confession of unforgiveness but finally, I was able to fully forgive. The joy of that journey and the release of the ledger I held against that person is so freeing. Like it says in 1 Corinthians 13:5, love "keeps no record of wrongs" (NIV).

Both confession and forgiveness have a powerful effect on us. Not only do they give us freedom but they also help us to

"lay aside every weight, and sin which clings so closely,

*and let us run with endurance the race that is set
before us" (Hebrews 12:1).*

We can run longer when we aren't carrying the sin and
unforgiveness that slows us down. Both confession and forgiveness are done in prayer and are things we should practice when
we spend time with God. Asking God to reveal any sin or unforgiveness in your heart is also another way to practice listening
to God.

———

PRAYER PRINCIPLE #6: CONFESS YOUR SIN AND FORGIVE EVERY DAY

To practice this: Sin is toxic. It leads to death, so we need to get it
out of our bodies as soon as possible. We can do this in two
ways:

1. Confess: Pray the Ten Commandments (Exodus 20)
   and Galatians 5:16–21 daily until you understand
   them and feel confident in doing a daily self-
   assessment. Ask God to reveal the sin and doubt in
   your heart and the times you didn't believe the truth
   of who he is. Remember 1 John 1:9 says, "If we confess
   our sins, he is faithful and just to forgive us our sins
   and to cleanse us from all unrighteousness." Then, be
   bold—confess your sins. Confess those sins like you
   are throwing out garbage! Step one is confessing to
   God. Step two is confessing to another Christian:
   "Therefore, confess your sins to one another and pray
   for one another, that you may be healed. The prayer of
   a righteous person has great power as it is working"
   (James 5:16).

2. Forgive: Think through your process of forgiveness. What does it look like? How can you practice forgiveness every day? Read these passages and write the benefits of forgiveness: Ephesians 4:32; Matthew 6:14, 18:21–22.

CHAPTER 7

PRINCIPLE SEVEN: MEDITATE ON TRUTH

Our cognitive ability is what makes us different from every other creature on the planet. Our mind is our superpower—it's how we work and thrive, but it can also be our weakness if we don't learn to properly tend to it. I've used quite a few plant analogies because God put so many in Scripture (ironic since I can't keep plants alive unless they are plastic). So to keep with that theme, let's say the mind is like a garden.

My husband and I purchased a home in Connecticut with a beautiful garden full of plants that were supposed to come back every year. We thought the upkeep would be minimal. It was not. A garden needs two things: someone to remove all the bad and someone to feed the good so it will grow. All the bad insects, diseases, or dead parts must be removed and then the plants must be fed with water, sunlight, fertilizers, and nutrients. If you don't remove the bad it slows the plant's growth or stops it completely and the plant simply starts to die. If a plant is not growing, it is dying.

Our home's welcome packet came with a referral for a yard

maintenance man who knew the yard. He had worked on it for years and planted many of the plants that continued to grow. He worked tirelessly year round to clean out the bad and upkeep the good, from weeding and mowing to sprinkler maintenance, fertilizing, and trimming trees to prevent too much shade, and more. It was a lot of work for him, but we were so thankful because we had the most beautiful garden that our family truly enjoyed.

Let's take this garden image and make it an analogy for our mind. Our minds take work. Cultivating a thriving mind is just like cultivating a flourishing garden—it takes work.

The mind is where we plant the seeds that grow into the fruits of the Spirit: the love, joy, peace, patience, kindness, goodness, faithfulness, gentleness, and self-control that we read about in Galatians 5:22–23.

There are two things that we need to do to have a thriving mind. Just like a thriving garden, we need to weed out the negative thoughts and replace them with positive thoughts. Sounds easy right? To be fair, once it becomes a habit it is, but just like any skill, it takes practice.

Negative thoughts function like disease, choking out our peace, joy, and mental health. These thoughts may include self-obsession, pride, anxiety, fear of man, anger, judgment, bitterness, complaining—you get the jist. Alternatively, positive thoughts allow for peace, joy, and other fruits to grow. Positive thoughts also include thinking about Scripture, thanksgiving, as well as talking and listening to God. In multiple places, Scripture lists negative things to *not* think about and then commands us to dwell on certain positive things. An example is given in Romans 1:28–31:

> *"They were filled with all manner of unrighteousness,*
> *evil, covetousness, malice. They are full of envy,*
> *murder, strife, deceit, maliciousness. They are*
> *gossips, slanderers, haters of God, insolent, haughty,*
> *boastful, inventors of evil, disobedient to parents,*
> *foolish, faithless, heartless, ruthless."*

On the opposite hand, Philippians 4:8 gives us a great list of positive categories of thought:

> *"Finally, brothers, whatever is true, whatever is honor-*
> *able, whatever is just, whatever is pure, whatever is*
> *lovely, whatever is commendable, if there is any*
> *excellence, if there is anything worthy of praise,*
> *think about these things."*

THE CIRCLES

When I was learning Spanish in college, my professor told us that it's tempting to think that language will develop in your mind like a word-for-word vocabulary list with English on one side and Spanish on the other. She warned us that this is not true. She drew a large circle on the white board and labeled it English and a smaller circle and labeled it Spanish. She told us that as you learn more of the language, the Spanish circle will grow but you go back and forth between the different circles when you switch languages. This is true of the flesh and Spirit as well. Before we are saved, we all function fully in the flesh circle (our native language). When we get saved, we develop in our mind a spirit circle (our newly learned language), but we fall back to the flesh circle when we walk in sin. When we confess our sin and repent, we re-enter the spirit circle. When we spend time dwelling on things of the flesh, the flesh circle grows. When we gain control of our negative thoughts, the flesh circle shrinks.

Likewise, when we dwell on Scripture, practice prayer, confession, encouragement, and meditate on truth the spirit circle grows.

Take a moment to inventory your thoughts. How often does your mind bend toward negative or flesh thoughts? How much do you fight to feed your mind with the positive or Spirit? Romans 8:6 says,

> *"For to set the mind on the flesh is death, but to set the mind on the Spirit is life and peace."*

MEDITATION

Thinking deeply about anything (positive or negative) is called meditation. We all meditate. All it is, is thinking intentionally and deeply about something. The national Library of Medicine says that "meditation usually refers to a formal practice that can calm the mind and enhance awareness of ourselves, our minds and our environment. Meditation in its many guises has been practised over millennia by diverse groups of people in many different traditions."[1] This includes Islam, Buddhism, Hinduism, and many others. The fact that so many religions have discovered the power of meditation is proof that there is benefit in removing distraction and negative thoughts from our minds. Even secular counselors suggest this as a solution for stress. If prayer is the conversation and relationship with God, then meditation is when we absorb the benefits of that conversation and relationship. Prayer and meditation are our hand-in-hand partners along our journey to becoming thriving Christians.

God's command for us to meditate is in Joshua 1:8:

> *"This Book of the Law shall not depart from your mouth, but you shall meditate on it day and night,*

*so that you may be careful to do according to all that
is written in it. For then you will make your way
prosperous, and then you will have good success."*

This verse commands us to meditate on Scripture and promises a positive outcome. This creates in me a provocative thought: Scripture isn't enough on its own. We've got to meditate on it! The Lord comes in and activates Scripture when we pair it with prayer and meditation. This is a command with a promise: when we meditate on the truth of Scripture—"the Book of the Law"—we will be prosperous and successful. Translation: our mind garden will thrive and grow the fruit of the Spirit, which is love, joy, peace, patience, kindness, goodness, faithfulness, gentleness, and self-control.

Recently I read a book titled *God's Battle Plan for the Mind: The Puritan Practice of Biblical Meditation* by David W. Saxton. In it, Saxton talks about meditation being like the savoring and enjoyment of food.[2] Now, I love food, so this caught my attention. I did a little research and found that there are tons of medical articles online about how beneficial it is to slowly chew and savor your food. I found different medical and health websites all agree that chewing slowly helps you to better digest your food, absorb more nutrients and increases your overall satisfaction of the food you are eating.[3, 4]

This is meditation—enjoying the truths of Scripture, one bite at a time. It is like slowly savoring wagyu steak. It is how we get the full benefit and blessing of the Word. Sitting and meditating enables us to take in the full benefits of our relationship with God.

If meditation is clearing our mind and focusing on something, then we have already been practicing this through the book so far. In chapter one I gave the example of sitting and soaking in the bath. Soaking in God's presence is meditation. In chapter two, the three questions I ask when I'm studying God's Word are by nature helping me meditate on the Word. Then in chapter four when we talked about getting quiet and listening—this is the first step in meditation—removing the distractions. After our distractions are gone and we are sitting in silence we can then inventory our thoughts and start weeding through what is negative and what is positive. Leading us to the first three steps of meditation:

1. Remove distraction
2. Stop the negative thoughts
3. Practice positive thoughts

REMOVE DISTRACTION

We discussed the value of removing distractions in chapter four but to be fair, it is easier said than done. The first step here is acknowledging the distractions. For me it is TV, social media, the news and seeking my own comfort. These things distract me. If I pick up my phone in the morning before I pick up my Bible, it is easy for me to skip my morning prayer and Bible study time. The habit of removing distraction is powerful on its own, but the next two steps supercharge it.

STOP THE NEGATIVE THOUGHTS

I still remember the day my husband and I decided I would stay at home full time with our children. It was tragic for me; I had the best job of my adult life, and I didn't want to quit. But after our second child was born, I didn't really have a choice. She had some health issues and would not take a bottle. Every time I left her, she would scream for four to five hours. Even though my husband is a parenting pro, nothing he tried would calm her down. I tell you this because the last day I worked at my job was the first day I started struggling deeply with the identity of being a stay-at-home mom.

Full-time stay-at-home moms were somewhat of a norm where we lived in Texas, but when we moved to Manhattan four years later, I knew only one other full-time mom. The weight of insecurity and shame plagued my mind. I was constantly comparing myself to my mom friends who had jobs out in the "real world." I worked nonstop around the house and constantly felt like I had to cook every meal and keep everything spotless. I stressed myself out trying to prove my value. The lie I constantly spoke over myself (and yes, it's embarrassing to admit) was that I was not adding anything of value to society. I believed I was less important because I didn't have a job or professional identity. To add insult to injury, people often said to me, "Oh so you are **just** a stay-at-home mom." Yes—Lacey Rozell is "just" a stay-at-home mom. I never voiced these negative beliefs about myself to anyone but my husband. Though he did his best to encourage me, I spoke the negative thoughts more regularly and more loudly than his sweet encouragements.

The tipping point was on Valentine's Day; one month before Covid shut down New York City. My husband and I went to a fancy sushi place to celebrate. Per the norm in Manhattan at the time, the tables were very close together making it nearly impossible to ignore the people beside us. Scott and I were seated next to two men who were clearly having a business dinner. We quickly gathered that one of the men was a jerk. I overheard him belittle and speak crassly of other employees and talk down to and manipulate the man with whom he was dining.

Barely into the meal I excused myself to use the restroom. While I was gone Scott and the two men exchanged pleasantries and job information and apparently Scott mentioned that I stay home with our children. Their conversation quickly faded as I returned. Scott and I were enjoying our Valentine's dinner when he also excused himself to the restroom. In Scott's absence the fun began! (Yes, I'm being sarcastic.) The jerk waited until Scott was out of earshot and said to me, "So how does it feel to not contribute financially to your family?"

I was in complete, jaw-on-the-floor shock. This guy did it— he said out loud the secret words of my mind that I constantly spoke over myself. But something clicked inside of me when he said them. For some reason, these words were okay for me to say, but they weren't okay for him to say! In that moment, I realized that if this jerk judged me and said negative things about me, how big of a jerk am I that I would say the same things to myself? I would never copy any of his other mannerisms, why would I believe what he says about me?

As I have mentioned before, I am not the quiet, gentle, or gracious type. Ready to battle, I dropped eye contact with the jerk and shifted my gaze to his dinner companion.

I calmly said, "Are you vouching for this guy?"

Poor fellow choked out, "Nope."

Scott returned, and the men shifted back to their own conversation. Obviously, the jerk was only interested in trying to intimidate me when I was alone, or he was too much of a coward to do it with my husband there. But it didn't work. Scott told me later that when he returned, they both looked terrified of me.

At the end of their meal, the two men began to argue over who would pay. I shocked Scott when I pointed at the jerk and said, "He's got the bill."

The two men glanced uneasily at each other and followed my command. When they got up to leave the jerk bent down and whispered to me, "You cost me a dinner."

I replied loudly with the sass that the situation required, "Your mouth cost you that dinner."

Scott stared at me in disbelief. After they left, I told him the tale. I confessed that when the jerk spoke my secret words of condemnation out loud it triggered something inside of me. I decided from then on, I was no longer going to believe them.

I, of course, am in no way suggesting that anyone get into verbal altercations with strangers, but I am suggesting that we aggressively stand firm against the lies in our mind. If I won't let anyone else accuse me of something, how can I stand by when I do it to myself? We are our own worst critic and the person we listen to the most. This scenario made me realize the power of truth; when I fought the jerk, I fought myself. I now see negative thoughts as an enemy to be conquered; an enemy I can defeat easily with truth.

In our home, if my daughter says, "I am so terrible at this. I stink," I respond, "Don't you dare talk about my daughter like that!"

When negative thoughts come, confess them out loud and counter them with the truth. The truth for me—Lacey Rozell the stay-at-home mom—is: "I am a valuable part of society. God has called me to stay home with these kids and I will do my best. I will not define myself by what others say or think about me. I am loved, valuable, and I love being a stay-at-home mom!" What is the truth to the lies you're telling yourself?

We can focus on the negative but it's just like the expression "Miss the forest for the trees." Negative thoughts blind us to the whole picture. We only have so many hours in a day. Focusing on the negative steals time from our positive thoughts.

THE BATTLE BETWEEN NEGATIVE AND POSITIVE THOUGHTS

The battle between negative and positive thoughts over space in your mind is REAL. An example of this for me is that right now I am experiencing significant back pain. It has been going on for about a week. If I am not careful, I will just say over and over:

"My back hurts."

"This stinks."

"I hate this."

Or in all honesty I will distract myself with TV. Which does not help me, in fact it leaves me miserable and not productive.

This weekend I had a planned trip to California for a wedding. Despite my pain, I attended along with my daughters and long-time friend Kelly. Kelly is obnoxiously optimistic. I say "obnoxious" sarcastically but also seriously; her optimism annoys the pessimist in me. She literally cheers and is excited about everything: the snacks in Comfort Plus, the beds in the hotel, the presentation at the restaurant, everything is "Awesome." When I looked back at our weekend, I realized something—I couldn't sit and think about the pain I was in because her positivity bullied the negative thoughts right out of me. Removing negative thoughts isn't easy, but you can fight them with positive thoughts! Kelly did this for me over the weekend, but now that we are back home, I have to do this for myself.

One of the positive habits I have used is thankfulness. We will talk about it more in the next section but my battle plan against the crankiness that accompanies physical pain is to challenge myself by asking,

---

"What if everything I didn't thank God for today was gone tomorrow?"

This seemingly strange question has helped me spend the days running down the list of everything I want to keep in my life and telling God *Thank You*. It has brought so much joy and peace in this weird season of back pain!

PRACTICE POSITIVE THOUGHTS

I have found three simple yet powerful ways to meditate on positive thoughts. We know the Bible encourages us to meditate on Scripture, but what other thoughts should we be spending our time meditating on? Over and over in Scripture we are commanded to praise God and be thankful. (See Isaiah 12:4–5; Psalm 7:17 and 95:1–3.) Thanks and praise are two powerful habits that transform our minds to be aligned with God's point of view. They also help us to keep out the negative thoughts that tempt us to believe the lies of this world. For example, Psalm 100:4 says,

> *"Enter his gates with thanksgiving, and his courts with praise! Give thanks to him; bless his name!"*

Remember, when we are commanded to do something in Scripture, it is for our good. Just like when I make my kids eat protein and vegetables. I don't encourage them to eat these things because I like to make them do random acts of obedience to prove that I am boss; it is for their good! God is a good God, and praise and thanksgiving lead to a thriving, fruit-producing mind!

PRAISE

Praise is one of those actions that seems like it is only good for the recipient. It isn't. Praise benefits both the praise-r and the praised. When we praise God, it aligns us with the truth of who He is and who we are. Both are important.

My husband and I spent the first ten years of our marriage living in the same town we grew up in. When we moved to New York City I learned the value of Apple Maps as well as City Mapper (an app that helps you navigate the subway and bus systems). I always had one of those apps on because not only do they show where you are going, but they show where you are. You cannot reach a destination if you don't know from where you're starting. For me this is one of the major benefits of praise. When we say, "Our father who art in heaven, hallowed be your name," it is a reminder that God is sitting on the throne, he is worthy of worship or "hallowing" because he is in complete power and authority. This is my "father" therefore I am his daughter, and I can call on him at any time. He is eager and listening, I am valued and loved. If I start here, it is so much easier to get anywhere I want to go. Praise helps us to realign ourselves with the truth, so we aren't believing or walking in lies.

THANKSGIVING

Even non-biblical scholars remark on the many benefits linked to thanksgiving. An article written by Kristin Francis MD, a psychiatrist at Huntsman Mental Health Institute, states, "Expressing gratitude can positively change your brain. It boosts dopamine and serotonin, the neurotransmitters in the brain that improve your mood immediately, giving you those positive feelings of pleasure, happiness, and well-being."[5]

In my experience, thanksgiving is an easy way to shut down complaining. Complaining makes me feel angry and robs my peace, so I try my best not to do it. Thanksgiving realigns us, gives us peace and joy, and protects us from toxic thoughts like ungratefulness, greed, and lust. I can sit and think about everything I don't have, or I can dwell on the things I do have. Thanksgiving also helps us acknowledge that God is the giver of good gifts, and we can pray and ask him for what we need.

Once we remove distraction and stop the negative thoughts we can focus on the three ways to practice positive thought:

1. Read and think about Scripture
2. Think about how amazing God is—aka Praise God
3. Intentionally practice thankfulness

———

PRAYER PRINCIPLE #7: MEDITATE ON TRUTH

Take time to prayerfully inventory your thoughts. Draw the two circles for yourself: the flesh circle and the spirit circle. As you go through your day write down your thoughts in each circle. Which circle do most of your thoughts fall into? Make a plan to dwell on things of the Spirit throughout your day. This is hard! But when we plan, it becomes easier. Remember the verse from Romans 8:6,

"For to set the mind on the flesh is death, but to set the mind on the Spirit is life and peace."

———

1. Behan, C. "The Benefits of Meditation and Mindfulness Practices During Times of Crisis Such as Covid-19." *Irish Journal of Psychological Medicine*, U.S. National Library of Medicine, Dec. 2020, www.ncbi.nlm.nih.gov/pmc/articles/PMC7287297/.
2. Saxton, David W. *God's Battle Plan for the Mind: The Puritan Practice of Biblical Meditation*. Reformation Heritage Books, 2020.
3. "7 Important Benefits of Chewing Your Food." *OPEX Fitness*, OPEX Fitness, 25 Aug. 2023, www.opexfit.com/blog/benefits-chewing-food.
4. Zelman, Kathleen M. "Crunch! Chew Your Way to Healthier Eating." *WebMD*, WebMD, www.webmd.com/obesity/features/crunch-chew-your-way-to-healthier-eating. Accessed 1 Sept. 2023.
5. "Practicing Gratitude for Better Health and Well-Being." *University of Utah Health | University of Utah Health*, 6 Nov. 2023, healthcare.utah.edu/health-feed/postings/2021/11/practicing-gratitude.php.

CHAPTER 8

INTERCESSION

"Yes! Uno!" I yelled at Stephanie.

"No!" she responded, "you have to say it when one of us has one card left. I have three, you have five, and Kim has two!"

Stephanie was my best friend when we were six. Her sixteen-year-old sister Kim was teaching us how to play Uno. Clearly, I didn't understand the rules, so I kept shouting at the wrong time. Kim wanted to be a teacher and said that teaching us games was good practice. Steph and I loved her and thought she was so cool, so we were her willing pupils. I remember hours and hours of us laughing, clapping, and playing. Not only was Kim nice but she had the coolest room. I would stare in awe at the novels on her shelf, the TV with all the VHS movies, the stereo in the corner and, of course, her New Kids on the Block poster beside her bed.

Kim and Stephanie lived down the street from me and I wandered to their house often. That day as we sat learning how to play Uno, we could hear the stereo blaring in the other room. It was loud enough that we didn't really hear much else going on in the rest of the house. But suddenly the music stopped. At that moment we noticed there was a loud commotion in the other room—really loud. Kim quickly stood up when she realized something that my six-year-old self didn't realize. Her mom and dad were fighting, and the noise was moving our way.

Without warning and for some reason unbeknownst to me, Kim shoved Stephanie and me off the bed, game forgotten, and into a corner. Just then their mom fled into the room clearly hoping for solace. Kim grabbed her mother's arms. They looked like two soldiers preparing a line of defense. To my surprise Kim stood in front of her mom as if to cut off her dad's anger. I thought surely he wouldn't hurt Kim, but as I was huddled in the corner with Stephanie I watched as their dad raged into the room and shoved Kim aside. Fear flashed through both women's eyes and that was when the fight became physical.

Steph's dad grabbed her mom by the throat and shoved her onto Kim's bed. The force knocked down the New Kids on the Block poster when her head crashed a hole into the wall. As the poster fell, I realized it covered two similar holes. *Oh my gosh! Had this happened before?* my six-year-old mind raced as my body froze. My eyes went to Kim. I saw her sixteen-year-old face shift from fear to determination. She quickly jumped into action and tackled her dad, knocking him over. Her heroics released the grip he had on her mom's neck and the fight ended. Kim had interceded.

Instantly my perception of Kim changed from thinking she was cool to knowing she was a hero. She calmly scooped up Stephanie and me and told us that it was time to go to my house to play. Kim walked us safely to my house and when she said goodbye, I noticed her hands shaking. I never saw their dad again and no one ever spoke a word about that day. But clearly —three decades later—it was an incident I could never forget.

Kim did teach me that day; she taught me bravery and she was my childhood hero.

INTERCESSION

Intercession is the act of intervening on behalf of another.[1] Intercessory prayer is standing in the gap for another. We see three types of intercessory prayer play out in Scripture. The first is defensive intercession and it is a lot like the situation above. When we see someone who needs defending or rescuing, we pray for them. When someone is sick or in a situation that they cannot get themselves out of, we petition the God of the universe who can in fact deliver them. He can and will hear our cry.

The second type is that when we pray for others we step in as their advocate. It is like what Esther did for the Israelite people in the Book of Esther. She had the ear of the king and she interceded and advocated for her people. When we pray for one another and go to God with petitions for them, we are advocating on their behalf.

The third part of intercession is message delivery. This is what the prophets did in the Old Testament: they prayed, God spoke, and they were responsible for delivering the message to God's people. Even though we are not necessarily prophets, we are commanded to pursue prophecy (see 1 Corinthians 14:1). In my experience the number one place I receive prophecy or words from God is when I am praying for others. I think it is actually more common than we think. When we pray for others and a verse, a message or an encouragement comes to our mind, this is a word from God. It is then our responsibility to prayerfully consider sharing it with the person we are praying for.

To break it down, the three parts of intercession are:

1. Defense
2. Advocate
3. Message delivery

Even though intercessory prayer doesn't involve you physically tackling someone, it is just as powerful because you are tackling issues in the spiritual realm. From an outside perspective, praying for others may seem like a powerless habit that weak people do as a last resort. I assure you; it is not. Intercessory prayer is basically petitioning the king of the universe on behalf of another. Intercessory prayer is more powerful than physical action because you have the power of the king of heaven behind you.

Intercessory prayer is like when my son pulls me aside and pleads for me to get his sister the ice horse from the movie *Frozen* that she wants for her birthday. He, my son, has an audience with me. He has a relationship with me, and he knows me and my love for his sister. He pleads to me on her behalf for what she wants and *needs*. It is the same with us when we go to our father God for our brother or sister. This is exactly how we bring praying for others into our first five prayer principles. Here is the list in case you need a reminder:

1. God Wants a Relationship with You
2. Know Your Bible
3. Know Your God
4. Listening in the Silence
5. The Posture of Humility and Submission
6. Confess and Forgive
7. Meditate on Truth

We have a relationship with God (principle one) and we know his character and his love for others because of what we learn in Scripture (principles two and three). When I pray for others, I have the most powerful experiences with principle four —to get quiet and listen (incredible story on this in the next section). Intercession also takes principle five—the posture of humility and submission—to a whole new level. When I hear a friend is struggling, my first instinct is to try to fix their problem myself, but I've learned that I first should submit their problem to God. James 5:16 says,

> *"Therefore, confess your sins to one another and pray for one another, that you may be healed. The prayer of a righteous person has great power as it is working."*

Prayer with others is where we practice confession and forgiveness. And when we meditate on truth, we can encourage and love others in a truth-filled way, like sharing Scripture or truths from Scripture.

PRAYING WITH AND FOR OTHERS

A few years back I was a member of a prayer team with an awesome group of people. We committed to praying together every Sunday morning before church and would see incredible things happen. One consistent theme was that we would hear words from God to encourage one another and the church. One of our regular attendees, Margie, was nine months pregnant. One Friday morning when I was doing meal prep for the day, I got a text message that still makes my eyes swell up with tears. It said, "Margie lost the baby, please pray." I fell to the floor half-crying and half-screaming. "No God, send her back! Send the baby back. Right now, in the name of Jesus heal this baby and give her back to Margie. I know you can!" I screamed until I was hoarse, then I just cried and listened.

My silence was God's opportunity, and he took it. He

showed me the most beautiful picture I have ever seen. I saw Jesus' face full of pain. He knelt beside me and it was like he was in full agreement with my sadness and felt the pain of Margie's loss more so than I did. But then his face changed, he looked down into his arms and his tears turned to pure, elated joy. His joy was like the joy I have only seen in pictures of moms when they hold their newborn for the first time. As I saw his face and his eyes drop to his arms, my eyes followed. In his arms was a beautiful, plump, healthy baby girl. He held her like I held my babies, neck craned, eye contact maintained and a smile that sends a shock of joy through anyone lucky enough to see it. As I watched the picture unfold Jesus took a step back, baby cradled tightly, and turned his back to me as he bounced the baby, speaking to her in soft whispers and began walking toward what looked like a crystal shimmering gate.

The trance broke and my joy turned back into screaming, "NO!!!! Bring her back!!! NO Jesus please!!!" I am sobbing now as I type this, but this is how Jesus comforted me as I prayed for my friend. I was angry but also felt a weird peace. When I went to visit my friend in the hospital the next day, I was really struggling with whether I should tell her about the vision. But finally, when we were alone, I heard a whisper—"Tell her." I was bold. I laid down my fear and I told her about what I saw. She grabbed my hands and cried. She said, "I know. I know Jesus has her, but I don't think I truly believed it until now."

I tell this story for two reasons: to share the beauty of praying with one another but to also challenge the doubt that often accompanies unanswered prayers. I have no idea why God allowed Margie's sweet baby girl to die. I am not going to pretend that it wasn't awful. It was.

But even when the prayer isn't answered the way we want, He. Is. Good.

That year taught me the power of intercessory prayer, spending an hour each Sunday in the small chapel of that church, and I have never forgotten it.

WHOSE LIFE WOULD CHANGE?

Let's look now at a few ways I have seen God work through prayer in community.

Years ago, my husband and I heard a quote on the Christian radio station *Air One* that has stuck with us. A preacher asked, "If all of your prayers were answered today would anyone's life change but yours?" At the time, I was in the middle of writing the class on prayer that led me to write this book. This question really challenged me to be more intentional with praying for others. I will say that up until that point I prayed for others regularly but not nearly as much as I prayed for myself. This quote provoked me to think long and hard on the topic of intercessory prayer or praying for others.

When I prayed for others, did I pray as if I wanted to change their life? Did I pray with the hope and belief that God could change even the worst of sinners into godly loving people? I am not making any assumptions about you, but I do know that this quote changed my prayer life. I now pray passionately as if I can impact the lives of others just by praying for them. I realized that if I taught others to pray like this, that even more people could be impacted. All to say, praying for others became a life-giving powerful tool that has changed me in so many ways. I want to see it do the same for you.

Eventually, my habit of praying for others spread beyond

my church community. When I would see an ambulance racing down the street or a homeless person or an angry person in the checkout line, I would pray for them—usually to myself. I just started secretly interceding for everyone. Soon I started bringing my kids into it when appropriate. For example, if I am honest, I used to see ambulances or fire trucks as an interruption to my day but now it is a chance to teach my kids to pray. When we see emergency vehicles, we stop and talk to God and ask him to help the hurt and give wisdom to the medics. One day my two-year-old was out on the playground at her preschool when an ambulance passed. She immediately started praying out loud and soon her teacher and classmates joined her. I got a tear-splattered note home that day that my two-year-old helped remind her adult teacher of the power of prayer and she could never view an ambulance siren the same again.

HOW I BENEFIT FROM INTERCESSION

There is one unexpected personal benefit of intercession. When I am stuck all up in my feelings or obsessing over something I am anxious about, I pray for others. When I am worried about what people think about me or fearful about some circumstance in my life, I pray for others. Basically, it protects me from selfishly thinking about myself. Philippians 2:3–5 says,

> "Do nothing from selfish ambition or conceit, but in humility count others more significant than yourselves. Let each of you look not only to his own interests, but also to the interests of others. Have this mind among yourselves, which is yours in Christ Jesus."

This act of selflessness makes us more like Christ! The little habit of intercessory prayer is beneficial to me because it does three things:

1. Takes my mind off myself
2. Puts me in conversation with God
3. Allows me to watch God work

INTERCEDING FOR SINNERS

A few weeks ago, during a stressful season of work for Scott, I had some complaints about how he was acting. He was working longer than usual hours and was tired and short with me and the kids. My grievances seem so much smaller right now as I write them, but they felt big at the time. One morning during my prayer time I vented my complaints to God and really felt like he sympathized and comforted me. I asked God to heal my relationship with Scott and then went about my day. I didn't say anything to Scott. A little while later my husband came to me with a joyful demeanor and apologized for how stressed he had been and said he didn't like how it was affecting the family. I was shocked! I later told Scott about how I had prayed that very morning for him. Scott said, "It is so encouraging to me that we have God as our advocate." This is what praying does. God will go before us and work on our behalf if we are willing to bring him into the conversation. Why don't we submit our problems and struggles to the God who can actually do something about them?

To illustrate how persuasive praying in community can be to God, I can't help but turn to another mommy moment with my three children. Upon the birth of our third child, my husband and I went from man-on-man defense to zone. We had three kids in three years and the kids quickly learned the art of working together for a common goal—also known as ganging up on us. One way we saw this play out was when my oldest daughter would come to me and ask to watch TV and I would say, "No, go play." She would leave the room and enlist her younger brother and sister to help her make a colorful sign that said "TV." The little three-soldier army would return smiling and proud of their artwork to ask again. They used this tactic a few times, and I will be honest it grew harder to say "No." Seeing my kids playing together and using teamwork to ask for something…it is one of my most favorite things! I am not saying this is exactly what is happening when we pray together, but I will say, the unity of my children making a petition definitely pulled on my heart strings. God is a good father; he loves his kids. I think he loves seeing us come together to pray.

I practice praying in community when I am physically with others, on the phone and through text messages. If I am having a down day and need prayer, I will text a friend and ask how I can pray for them and then type out the prayer right there. This helps me so much! And let me tell you, not once has anyone said, "No, you weirdo, I don't want you to pray for me," in over twenty years of me asking people if I can pray for them.

ASKING OTHERS TO PRAY

Asking others to pray is powerful, even if in the moment it feels like weakness. The times that I have asked for prayer, I have been blown away by how God moves. For example, my husband and I were blessed to live in the same city in Texas as both our parents and siblings. We were supported, loved, and blessed in so many ways by having family close by, especially when our children were young. When our youngest was two, we felt like God might be calling us to leave and move to New York City. It felt crazy, and honestly we were a little embarrassed to even mention it to anyone because we thought we would look foolish. One day we gathered up our courage and I texted the vaguest text I could to a prayer-warrior couple who were friends of ours. I said, "Hey can y'all pray for us? We have a decision to make, and we need God's direction." They responded "Sure." Shortly after, the husband also texted, "I heard something weird from the Lord and maybe it will make sense to you because it makes no sense to me. I heard the verse from Genesis 12:1: 'Go from your country and your kindred and your father's house to the land that I will show you.'" Scott and I sat and stared at that text in complete shock. Not only did our friends pray for us, but God spoke through them to give us the very direction we were asking for. And to answer your question, yes, we did obey and move. We left our family, our security, our babysitters, the only life we knew, and we went. Looking back now I can see all the ways this move changed our lives. I could fill a book on all the ways this prayer request and our move to NYC has made us different and better people.

PRAYING SCRIPTURE IS POWERFUL

When we study the Word (principle two), submit to the Word (principle five) and then meditate on the Word (principle seven) it quickly becomes a part of our thinking. When we learn Scripture like this, we can't help but see greater fruit and power in our prayer life. I challenge you to begin practicing praying Scripture back to God. It may seem so basic, but it is so powerful!

You can't go wrong when you pray Scripture—God's words are perfect. Even Jesus prayed Scripture.

As I have started this habit, I have realized that some of the fancy words I heard adults pray when I was a child were actually from Scripture. When someone would say, "Thy will be done" that is from the Lord's prayer in Matthew 6:10. Praying Scripture is using words that Christians have prayed for centuries. There is something beautiful about that.

When I married my husband, I gained an amazing sister-in-law, Leanne, who has become one of my most cherished friends. Leanne and I have had many conversations about prayer, and I know for a fact that she practices all the principles in this book. I am going to preface this next story by saying I have an extreme and somewhat dramatic personality. I am loud (usually too loud) and always excited and passionate about something. This can be a gift, but just like all our God-given personalities, gifts not properly submitted to God can also be a curse. I run into the latter often. I can be perceived as rude, arrogant, disrespectful, and even a bit offensive.

A few years ago, when I prayed about teaching a class on how to pray, I of course enlisted my prayer-warrior sister-in-law for prayer support. A few weeks in, Leanne told me that when she prayed for me, she had a specific verse come to mind. She said she had been praying that verse over me every morning. It was Philippians 4:5–7:

> "Let your reasonableness be known to everyone. The Lord is at hand; do not be anxious about anything, but in everything by prayer and supplication with thanksgiving let your requests be made known to God. And the peace of God, which surpasses all understanding, will guard your hearts and your minds in Christ Jesus."

Obviously, this is a great verse to support the class on prayer and lack of anxiousness that I had been praying for, but she said, "Actually, I specifically pray the part that says, 'Let your reason-ableness be known to everyone.'" You could have heard crickets in the room after she said this. She went on, "You know that in the NIV instead of *reasonableness* it says *gentleness*?" In my mind I thought, *Yes, and neither of those words have ever been used to describe me.* But I thanked her and prayed about what she said for a few days. In all honesty, I didn't want her verse to be for me because gentleness doesn't come easy to me.

While praying one day, I was reminded of the importance of unity in the church body. When I am loud and abrasive all the time, it can disrupt the peace and unity of others (even if it makes it fun). At this point, I started working on not restraining my personality but remembering that sometimes being quiet and gentle is important and beneficial to myself and others. It seems small, but this experience has truly impacted me. To this day, when I feel anxious or overly dramatic, this verse comes to mind. There is always a balance with the gifts God gives us, and this verse helps me remember to find mine.

Leanne could have told me to stop being such a loud drama queen (and she wouldn't have been wrong), but she didn't. What she did is what I am encouraging us to do: bring Scripture into our prayer life. Her steps were:

1. She prayed for me.
2. God revealed a verse to her.
3. She read that verse and prayed for me daily.
4. She shared that verse with me.
5. God used it to work on my heart.

This is what happens when we pray Scripture. God wants to love others through our interactions with them. When we submit to Him and pray His Word, our work becomes powerful and effective. There is power in Scripture like is says in Hebrews 4:12:

> *"For the word of God is living and active, sharper than any two-edged sword, piercing to the division of soul and of spirit, of joints and of marrow, and discerning the thoughts and intentions of the heart."*

Also Isaiah 55:11:

> *"So shall my word be that goes out from my mouth; it shall not return to me empty, but it shall accomplish that which I purpose, and shall succeed in the thing for which I sent it."*

There is power to do more than change our personal flaws. If God cares about walking with us through our flaws, what else does He care about and want to lead us through?

———

PRACTICE

Remember the challenge I received from the *Air One* radio preacher? Here is your chance to practice and accept the same challenge—to see whose life will change when you pray. Pick three people to pray for this week. Call and ask how you can pray specifically for them this week. Write it down. I use note cards. Ask God for a verse for them. If you can't think of one, look one up. Today my friend told me she was struggling with anxiety on a specific topic this week. So I Googled "Bible verses on anxiety" and I found:

> *"When the cares of my heart are many, your consolations cheer my soul"* (Psalm 94:19).

I wrote this on the back of her card, and I texted her, "This the verse I am praying over you this week."

Don't let yourself forget the power of praying for others and letting them pray for you! Although we may not be in a position to tackle one another's problems physically like Kim did in the opening story, our prayers are just as powerful. This is how we battle for one another, and this is an opportunity to watch God work and hear his voice.

---

1. "Intercession Definition & Usage Examples." *Dictionary.Com*, Dictionary.-com, www.dictionary.com/browse/intercession. Accessed 1 Sept. 2023.

CHAPTER 9
UNANSWERED PRAYERS

I will be honest. The first thing I think of when I hear the phrase "unanswered prayers" is the Garth Brooks song by the same name. In the song he tells the story of running into an ex and remembering how much he prayed he could be with her in high school, but then so grateful that he wasn't so he could find and marry his wife. The chorus goes:

> *"Sometimes I thank God for unanswered prayers*
> *Remember when you're talkin' to the man upstairs*
> *And just because He doesn't answer, doesn't mean He*
>   *don't care*
> *'Cause some of God's greatest gifts are unanswered*
>   *prayers"[1]*

Although there is truth in the lyrics, to me the phrase "unanswered prayer" is a little misleading because, to be fair, most of the time we get an answer. We just don't like the answer. So this section should be titled: "When We Pray and Don't Get What We Ask For" but since that doesn't quite roll off the tongue I will stick with "Unanswered Prayers." Unanswered prayers are a source of doubt for many believers. I want to take a short moment to explore the truth behind the concept and see what Scripture says about unanswered prayers.

RELATIONSHIP

When we boil it down, the real question seems to be: Do you believe God is good even if he doesn't give you the answer you want? Do you view God as a genie that you can control, or as a person that you are in relationship with? In chapter one we used a few parenting analogies to talk about our relationship with God. One of things I have learned as a parent is that it's ok if my kids don't always understand why I do or don't do things. I know that in my effort to be a good mom, I do what I believe is best, even if it's not always what my kids want.

In Luke 11 Jesus is teaching the disciples how to pray by introducing the Lord's prayer. He then reminds them and us that God is a good father by saying:

> "And I tell you, ask, and it will be given to you; seek, and
> you will find; knock, and it will be opened to you. For
> everyone who asks receives, and the one who seeks
> finds, and to the one who knocks it will be opened.
> What father among you, if his son asks for a fish, will
> instead of a fish give him a serpent; or if he asks for
> an egg, will give him a scorpion? If you then, who
> are evil, know how to give good gifts to your chil-
> dren, how much more will the heavenly Father give
> the Holy Spirit to those who ask him!" (vv. 9–13).

Jesus teaches us about God's character in this verse—he is a good father who gives good gifts. Based on this passage, what if a child asks for a poisonous serpent, would the father in this text give him one? No, he wouldn't. God's plan is perfect and good. When we ask for things, even seemingly good things, we don't see the whole picture or know that what we are asking for is not good for us or for others. To further solidify this point, in Jeremiah 29 God speaks through the prophet Jeremiah to his people who are in exile:

> "For thus says the LORD: When seventy years are
> completed for Babylon, I will visit you, and I will
> fulfill to you my promise and bring you back to this
> place. For I know the plans I have for you, declares
> the LORD, plans for welfare and not for evil, to give
> you a future and a hope. Then you will call upon me
> and come and pray to me, and I will hear you. You
> will seek me and find me, when you seek me with all
> your heart. I will be found by you, declares the
> LORD, and I will restore your fortunes and gather
> you from all the nations and all the places where I
> have driven you, declares the LORD, and I will bring
> you back to the place from which I sent you into
> exile" (vv. 10–14).

God sent his people into exile because their temporary comfort was so far less important than their salvation and eternal life in heaven. Second Corinthians 4:17–18 says:

> "For this light momentary affliction is preparing for us
> an eternal weight of glory beyond all comparison, as
> we look not to the things that are seen but to the
> things that are unseen. For the things that are seen
> are transient, but the things that are unseen are
> eternal."

Let's look at a modern-day example of this. Recently I had to take my kids to the dentist to get their cavities filled. I had flashbacks to some of the very traumatic experiences my children and I have had at doctors' offices. I remembered times when I had to hold my children down for a dentist or doctor to do something painful to them, but was also for their good. When my daughter was two, I had to lay on her to hold her still while the dentist pulled an abscessed tooth. She screamed, I cried, and even now the dentist and hygienist mark it as the most traumatic incident in their office.

Once when she was seven, I didn't hold her hands tight enough and she grabbed the needle when the doctor tried to give her the numbing shot before her treatment. It was bad. I, a good mom, hate taking my kids to the dentist. In fact, my husband, after doing it once, said he could never do it again. We hate it because we hate to see our children cry. We do it because it is what is best for them. They don't understand that; we do. So when she looks me straight in the eyes, with tears dripping down and says, "Please Mommy, I don't want to do this." I can't give her what she wants. I have to give her what she needs because a cavity left unchecked can lead to so many worse things. She doesn't understand that, just like we don't understand the full picture in comparison to God.

God is all-knowing. He knows what is best for us and those around us.

As his kids, we don't always get to know the whole story. We may not know why he allows hardship and death, but we do know he is good. The hard thing is, he is good even when we don't get what we pray for.

WHAT DOES THE BIBLE SAY?

I found two reasons in Scripture for why God doesn't answer prayers:

1. **Our sin:** "You ask and do not receive, because you ask wrongly, to spend it on your passions" (James 4:3). Also, Isaiah 59:2 says, "But your iniquities have made a separation between you and your God, and your sins have hidden his face from you so that he does not hear."
2. **God's glory:** "That the works of God might be displayed in him" (John 9:3). More on this verse in a moment.

Our sin is a relationship blocker, like I mentioned in chapter six. When we are walking in sin we are not aligned with God and therefore our actions and requests most likely will not fall under his will and plan for our life. God has a plan for us, he does listen to our requests, and we do have influence, but he will not change his plan if what we ask is not for his glory and our eternal good.

The disciples had read similar verses on sin and assumed that all unanswered prayers were caused by sin (see John 9). One day they were walking with Jesus and passed by a blind man begging. They asked,

> "'Rabbi, who sinned, this man or his parents, that he was born blind?' Jesus answered, 'It was not that this man sinned, or his parents, but that the works of God might be displayed in him'" (vv. 2–3).

Your sin can cause unanswered prayers, but all unanswered

prayers aren't caused by sin. To use an analogy from geometry: all squares are rectangles but not all rectangles are squares.

The notes in the ESV Study Bible on John 9:3 say that this verse "indicates that God in his mysterious and wise providence sometimes allows his children to go through hardship and suffering so that they can experience God's mercy and power in delivering them."[2] Malachi 3:6 tells us that God doesn't change. So, this is still true when God doesn't rescue us when we ask him to but allows us to walk through a hardship or endure unanswered prayers. In Psalm 23 he promises that when we do walk through a difficult time or "valley" he is there with us:

> *"Even though I walk through the valley of the shadow of*
> *death, I will fear no evil, for you are with me" (v. 4).*

So, does he intentionally allow us to walk through hard things? Yes. But will he leave us? No.

YOUR WILL BE DONE

In Luke 22 Jesus was praying in a garden before his arrest and execution and he made a request that wasn't granted. Jesus said,

> *"Father, if you are willing, remove this cup from me.*
> *Nevertheless, not my will, but yours, be done"*
> *(v. 42).*

You see, Jesus understood the assignment when he came to earth. He was to live a perfect life and then die for all our sins. That was all well and good until his thirty-three-year timer was up and it was time to do the hardest and most submissive thing that anyone in the history of the world has ever done—let his beloved chosen people kill him. The night before he died, the weight of the next day was so much that he sweated blood and then he cried out a prayer that was the only prayer we see him pray in Scripture that was not answered. He asked God to take the cup from him. I am going to point something out here, and I know it is a hard pill to swallow because I am wrestling with some unanswered prayers right now, but Jesus' unanswered prayer led to our salvation. If Jesus' prayer was answered—we would still be slaughtering cows and doves to atone for our sins. Jesus' unanswered prayer led to the salvation and forgiveness of anyone in the world who will receive it. That is the ultimate fulfillment of Romans 8:28:

> *"And we know that for those who love God all things work together for good, for those who are called according to his purpose."*

Did it still hurt? Yep. Would he wish it on anyone else? Nope. But God can use our unanswered prayers for good.

Far too many people unplug from God when they feel their prayers aren't answered, when life gets hard, when they lose the baby, watch a loved one die, or don't get healed. I am not going to pretend to know the theological answer to why God answers prayers sometimes and doesn't other times. I am going to encourage you with this:

1. Circumstances stink.
2. God hates watching his children hurt.
3. Jesus understands the pain of unanswered prayers.

MY UNANSWERED PRAYER

When I look around at my life today, I am so grateful that God said no to a few things I begged for. When I was twenty-two and graduating from college, my college pastor encouraged me to apply for a job in Atlanta, Georgia. The job was at a church doing women's ministry which was my dream job—or so I thought. I begged God for this job, I stepped out in faith and didn't even apply for anything else because I just knew God was going to say yes. Then lo and behold, after weeks of interviews and phone calls, right before my last college final, I got a call from the hiring pastor who let me know he was going with someone else. I was devastated and confused. Not only did I not have a backup plan, but my lease was also up in two weeks and the only place I had to go was back home to my parents' house. This felt like failure. I was down and defeated, but I packed my things and headed home.

I remember unloading the last box of my belongings into my sister's old room (she had taken over mine when I left) and crumbling into the corner chair. I grabbed my journal and in giant sloppy letters I wrote "WHY GOD WHY??" The last place on the planet I wanted to be was back in my hometown with no plans, no job leads and no money. But there I was angry, confused, and directionless. After a few days of moping around, my mom encouraged me to do a Bible study that was starting that week. I went…begrudgingly.

That night I met a woman named Diann who became my accountability partner. Not only did we walk through the Bible study together, but she also helped me get my teaching certificate. As I started the process of finding a teaching job, Diann was going through a divorce and invited me to live with her. Her only contingency was that her youngest son was away at college but would be home during holidays. If you haven't guessed it yet, her youngest son is my husband, Scott. Nope, he wasn't what I prayed for. He smoked, he partied, and he is younger than me.

When he came home for the holidays it was clear that he liked me, and to be honest I liked him, but he wasn't what I had prayed for. I wish I could say that the day I met him I knew he was the reason all my prayers weren't answered and we immediately began a Hallmark fairy tale life. But that's not how it went. I remember praying at night and telling God no.

"I see what you are doing God, and I don't think he is right for me."

I remember staring at the ceiling and hearing God loud and clear, "What if you don't know as much as I do? What if Scott is the best thing for you?"

I cried hot tears that night as God spoke to me his plans for Scott. I won't share those here, but I will tell you that everything God promised about Scott and the godly man he would become did come true. He is absolutely the best earthly thing that has happened to me. One of the first times we hung out, Scott told me that he had never heard anyone talk about Jesus the way I did. He was chasing after God and trying to leave behind the path he chose in college. He had a different past than me. God was bringing him out of a life of rebellion and into a life of obedience. God used Scott's past to begin to loosen my grip on legalism. Scott hadn't been perfect but God was good and working on both of our imperfections. I wouldn't change our story. We are best friends, run a successful company together, parent three amazing kids and live a life of joy and laughter…all because God said no to that job in Atlanta. I couldn't even dream to ask for the life I have now, yet God gave it to me anyway.

And just to clarify I have had God say no to other things that I didn't get to see play out like this Atlanta story.

I have had God tell me no and I still don't understand why, but he is good.

CONCLUSION

To wrap all this up, when we make requests to God the three possible answers he gives us are: yes, no, or not right now. Our prayers go unanswered because of our sin or God's will. These two reasons aren't always clear but the best way to heal from the hurt of unanswered prayers is in God's arms, not away from him.

My final challenge for us on the topic of unanswered prayers is this: Do you want God, or do you want what he can do for you? I have been guilty so many times of desiring what God can do for me more than wanting him.

I felt convicted of this years ago when I read Timothy Keller's book, *Prodigal God*. It is a quick and easy read, but man is it dense. Dr. Keller dissects the passage of Luke 15:11–32. In the text Jesus is addressing a mixed crowd of sinners and religious leaders teaching them through a parable about a wealthy father with two sons.

One son—the historically more famous of the two—was the prodigal who disrespected his father and demanded his inheritance early. His father obliged and the son squandered the money on debaucherous living. It was not until he was broke and working as a servant feeding pigs that he came to his senses. He was so hungry he envied the pigs' slops and decided to return to his father.

The customary reading of the text focuses on the father's response when he sees his prodigal son returning. The gracious and loving father (who represents God) forgets all decorum and runs to receive his son. This action communicates the love, grace, forgiveness, and restoration that all prodigals can find in our heavenly father's arms. But Dr. Keller digs deeper than the customary reading and points out that the story isn't over.

As the welcome party band plays, the older brother sulks outside. The loving father greets his oldest son with all the same grace and love for his younger son, but the older son's response is shocking. In verses 28–30 we see the older son's ungrateful fit. The text says,

> *"But he was angry and refused to go in. His father came out and entreated him, but he answered his father, 'Look, these many years I have served you, and I never disobeyed your command, yet you never gave me a young goat, that I might celebrate with my friends. But when this son of yours came, who has devoured your property with prostitutes, you killed the fattened calf for him!'"*

It is easy to see the prodigal son's sin, but the older son's sin is harder for us to spot. Dr. Keller said it perfectly: "It is not his sins that creates the barrier between him and his father, it's the pride he has in his moral record....He [the older son] was just as resentful of the father as the younger son. He, too, wanted the father's goods rather than the father himself. However, while the younger brother went far away, the elder brother stayed close and 'never disobeyed.' That was his way to get control. His unspoken demand is, 'I have never disobeyed you! Now you have to do things in my life the way I want them to be done.'"[3]

This line shocked me when I first read it because this was me. I viewed God as a vending machine; I put my good works in to get what I wanted out. But as Dr. Keller points out, "Neither son loved the father for himself. They both were using the father for their own self-centered ends rather than loving, enjoying, and serving him for his own sake."[4]

What a shock! Even when we want good things, we cannot see what the all-knowing God of the universe sees. If we reject him when he doesn't answer our prayers, we are doing exactly what the older brother from this story did. We want God's stuff and not him. How we view unanswered prayer is how we view

God. Is he still good even if I have a miscarriage? Is he still good even if I'm single? Is he still good if I get fired?

I will end with this: our God is good and he is God, we are not. In the beginning of the book, on page one, Dr. Keller defines "prodigal" as:

1. Recklessly extravagant
2. Having spent everything

Our God is a prodigal God. He is "recklessly extravagant" and spends everything on us—not even withholding his one and only son. This is true even when we don't get what we want.

Do you view God as a vending machine? Do you feel that if you put in your good works you should expect what you want out? Or is God your father and friend? May we take to heart the father's words in the story:

> *"And he said to him, 'Son, you are always with me, and*
> *all that is mine is yours'" (v. 31).*

My challenge for us is this: Who is God even when bad things happen or we don't get our prayers answered? Answer this question for yourself and sit with God in your grief. He may say no, but He will never leave you.

---

1. Garth Brooks. *No Fences*. Capitol Records, 1990.
2. ESV Study Bible, p 2041.
3. Keller, "Prodigal", pp. 35-36
4. pg. 36

CHAPTER 10
THE THRIVING VINE

Now that we have our seven principles in our tool belt, it's time to become experts at using them. Remember when I mentioned Einstein's attributed quote? "If anyone spends 15 minutes a day learning something new, in a year, he [or she)] will be an expert; in 5 years, a national expert."[1] One day of using these tools, probably won't change you—just like one day of studying a new language won't make you fluent, one day of basketball practice won't make you Lebron James, one day of lifting weights, one day of eating well, one day of studying science—no champion, thought leader, scientist or expert in any field became who they are in one day, one week or even one month—success takes consistency over months and even years. To fold this into our reference from John 15, to become a thriving grapevine, the vine has to stay connected to the branch. Thriving is achieved through consistency. We need consistency in our prayer life.

THE LIGHTBULB

Imagine I am standing in a dark room, holding a lightbulb. If connected to a power source, the lightbulb could illuminate the room. However, in my hand, disconnected from the power source, it can do nothing to dispel the room's darkness. In fact, it too is consumed by the darkness. If I screw the bulb into a lamp that is plugged into an electrical outlet the lightbulb will produce light, thus blessing me and anyone else in the room with the ability to see. But first I must connect it to the power source.

We Christians are like the lightbulb. We are created for a purpose—to illuminate a dark world—but we can only fulfill that purpose when we are in constant connection with God.

The image of a lightbulb also mirrors the image of the vine and the branches that we looked at in John 15. In verse 5 Jesus tells his disciples,

> "I am the vine; you are the branches. Whoever abides in
> me and I in him, he it is that bears much fruit, for
> apart from me you can do nothing."

Being apart from God is just like the unplugged lightbulb. If we aren't plugged in or "abiding," we aren't able to bear "much fruit." How do we stay in constant connection with God? Through prayer!

My heart's desire in writing this book is to help Christians cultivate their relationship with God—our power source, our vine. Just as God promised Abram in Genesis 12:2, we will thrive and "be a blessing" to others when we consistently stay connected to him. We do this through the seven principles in this book; we make them habits and then those habits will transform us into thriving fruit-producing Christians.

DAVID THE HERO

David is not only a biblical hero but a historical hero. Even outside of Scripture his bravery in fighting Goliath is known worldwide. But David didn't just wake up one day and decide to be a hero. David's bravery to fight against Goliath was trained into him; his habits led him to that moment. You see, for years David had watched over sheep. He was a shepherd who provided for and defended sheep. Not only did he fight off bears and lions, but he spent countless hours in prayer. Day in and day out as he watched his sheep, he wrote songs of worship to God. Over and over, he spoke words of truth to himself like:

> *"The Lord is my shepherd; I shall not want....I will fear no evil, for you are with me" (Psalm 23:1,4).*

> *"The Lord is my light and my salvation; whom shall I fear?" (Psalm 27:1).*

> *"I love you, O LORD, my strength. The LORD is my rock and my fortress and my deliverer, my God, my rock, in whom I take refuge, my shield, and the horn of my salvation, my stronghold. I call upon the LORD, who is worthy to be praised, and I am saved from my enemies" (Psalm 18:1–3).*

David had a relationship with God—this all-powerful, loving, and protective God. And David knew that God loved Israel (see Genesis 12, Psalm 47:4, Malachi 1:2–3, 1 Kings 10:9).

We read in 1 Samuel 17:8–10 that when David heard about a Philistine giant taunting the army of God, David didn't hesitate to volunteer to fight him. Ironically, David wasn't even supposed to be there. He wasn't a soldier. David happened to be there because he was on an errand for his father, delivering food to his older brothers who were soldiers in the battle (v. 17).

When David heard the taunts of the Philistine giant, David retorted,

> *"Who is this uncircumcised Philistine, that he should defy the armies of the living God?" (v. 26).*

As a mom of a boy, I can't help but chuckle that one of the first things David verbally attacked was the giant's...ahem... lack of circumcision. That's the human nature I see, but in a spiritual sense David's taunt was less about the ahem body part and more about the covenant position of the Israelites with God. Circumcision was a sign of God's covenant with the Hebrew people. David was pointing out the fact that some random guy, no matter how tall he is, is not a chosen Israelite protected and loved by God. Therefore, said man—or giant—didn't stand a chance.

You see, David had spent years focusing on how big God is. He knew that Goliath was small in comparison to God. The Israelite army, however, was focused only on themselves and their own strength. In comparison to one soldier, Goliath was enormous and undefeatable. I see the scene play out in my mind: David is in a tent telling Saul he will fight. He stands firm and confident as Saul frantically tries to talk him out of it. His confidence doesn't shake. Saul calls his armor bearer to bring his own armor, shield, and sword for David, but David refuses to use the unfamiliar protection. With a knowing smile on his face, David leaves the tent, not making eye contact with the soldiers or his brothers who were gathered outside. As they part to let him pass, he hears their whispers:

"He can't do this."

"That wimpy kid will die for sure. What is he thinking?"

Then his brother's start arguing among themselves, "If we don't stop him, Dad will kill us!"

To drown out the whispers and block out the doubt, David closes his eyes and remembers a psalm he wrote:

> *"I lift up my eyes to the hills. From where does my help*
> *come? My help comes from the LORD, who made*
> *heaven and earth" (Psalm 121:1–2).*

A smile fills his face. In slow motion, he continues to walk. He stops to grab his humble shepherd's pack to remove his weapon of choice: a simple sling. Then as he heads to a nearby stream, his brothers exhale, "Maybe he's running back to Daddy?" But no, David stoops down and picks out five smooth stones from the streambed. Never looking back, he continues toward the battlefield singing songs of praise to God the whole way,

> *"He will not let your foot be moved; he who keeps you*
> *will not slumber….the LORD will keep you from all*
> *evil; he will keep your life" (Psalm 121:3,7).*

With that promise on his lips and a sling in his hand, he cast the first stone.

There was nothing new about any of David's actions that day—they were his practiced habits of praise and bravery. But that day the world saw the man that God had been secretly forming out on the lonely hills with the sheep. The world saw the hero—the humble, faithful, bold hero.

This is the power of knowing the truth of who God is. God

doesn't change just because your circumstances do. David saw that fear had captivated the hearts of the Israelite army, but he was not deterred. The story says:

> And David said to Saul, "Let no man's heart fail because of him [Goliath]. Your servant will go and fight with this Philistine." And Saul said to David, "You are not able to go against this Philistine to fight with him, for you are but a youth, and he has been a man of war from his youth." But David said to Saul, "Your servant used to keep sheep for his father. And when there came a lion, or a bear, and took a lamb from the flock, I went after him and struck him and delivered it out of his mouth. And if he arose against me, I caught him by his beard and struck him and killed him. Your servant has struck down both lions and bears, and this uncircumcised Philistine shall be like one of them, for he has defied the armies of the living God." And David said, "The LORD who delivered me from the paw of the lion and from the paw of the bear will deliver me from the hand of this Philistine." (1 Samuel 17:32–27).

Like I said, when David grabbed his sling that day, he grabbed a tool he had used countless times to protect his sheep and he prayed to a God that he knew would deliver him. The discipline and consistency of David's prayer life and fighting off enemies led him to that day. He won and became a household name because of the hundreds of days before—not just for that one fight. David is a hero, and he is one worth emulating. If you read through 1 and 2 Samuel as well as seventy-five of the Psalms that he wrote, you will see that David walked in all seven prayer principles we've discussed in this book:

God Wants a Relationship with You: David had a relationship with God. David knew the hard work of being a good shepherd. He knew how the sheep depended on him and he had that same dependence on God. He wrote:

> *"The* LORD *is my shepherd; I shall not want. He makes*
> *me lie down in green pastures. He leads me beside*
> *still waters. He restores my soul" (Psalm 23:1–3).*

Know Your Bible: David knew the Word. He literally wrote seventy-five psalms. These are complementary to the Torah (first five books of the Bible). David would have been taught these books as a child as they were used to lead the Hebrew people in worship. He also would have had access to them as king. We see in Psalms so much truth about who God is.

Know Your God: As you read the Psalms you can see God's character through David's words. In Psalm 3:3–4 he says,

> *"But you, O* LORD, *are a shield about me, my glory, and*
> *the lifter of my head. I cried aloud to the* LORD, *and*
> *he answered me from his holy hill."*

Get Quiet and Listen: Out in the fields with the sheep David had hours upon hours of quiet time with God. Clearly, he listened to God because he wrote seventy-five psalms that are rich in spiritual truth.

The Posture of Humility and Submission: One of the most telling examples of this is in 1 Samuel 24. Saul was chasing after David and went into a cave to relieve himself, not knowing that David was hiding in the cave. In verse 4, David's men encouraged him to kill Saul by saying God had delivered Saul into David's hand, but David refused to kill Saul. He even reprimanded himself for cutting off a corner of Saul's robe, saying,

> *"The* LORD *forbid that I should do this thing to my lord, the* LORD'S *anointed" (v. 6).*

David refused to kill Saul simply because Saul was God's chosen king. The amazing part that really shows David's deep submission to God is the fact that David had been anointed to be the new king by Samuel the prophet of God. David knew God had rejected Saul as king and was preparing him to take over the throne. That's why Saul was actively trying to kill him. David chose to submit to God's plan and not his own.

Confess Your Sins and Forgive Every Day: David was the greatest king of Israel and called a man after God's heart (Acts 13:22), but he wasn't perfect. During a season of inconsistency David fell into some pretty terrible sin. While his army was away at war, David stayed home. One night he saw a woman bathing on the roof of her house, and he decided he had to have her. He lusted after Bathsheba, slept with her (it is actually argued that it was rape), and then had her husband killed so he could marry her. David was absolutely guilty of all these horrible things. As the king, he could have gotten away with it, but in his grace, God sent the prophet Nathan to gently convict David. David could have dismissed Nathan and avoided confession because he was king, but he confessed and repented. Once again, he shows that he was a godly man even though he was a sinner. In Psalm 51 he leaves us a wonderful example of how to confess our sins. We are all guilty and in need of a savior. God forgives us but we have to confess and admit we are wrong when we sin. Just like David did.

Meditate on Truth: In Psalm 119:97 David writes,

> *"Oh how I love your law! It is my meditation all the day."*

David mentions truths like this throughout the Psalms. As a

humble and godly man, he knew his desperate need for the truths of Scripture. He also said in Psalm 25:4–5:

> *"Make me to know your ways, O LORD; teach me your paths. Lead me in your truth and teach me, for you are the God of my salvation; for you I wait all the day long."*

The man who killed that giant practiced all these principles. My challenge for us is how do we develop these principles into habits? How do we train our minds and practice so much that when our day comes to defeat a goliath—whatever that giant may look like—nothing can stand in the way of our victory? The point is that consistency and staying connected to God leads to our thriving and our ability to fight well.

STAYING CONNECTED

Every relationship is unique. I have three children, and my relationship is a little different with each one of them. With one of my daughters, we like to get sushi together. With the other, I stroll through the bookstore. And with my son, I play sports; well, try anyways. The only thing that is consistent for all three kiddos is the time. Just like any relationship, staying connected to God takes time, togetherness, and conversation (prayer).

As I have challenged you in this book with specific ways to stay connected to God, which principles stand out to you? Which ones come easy and which ones take more discipline? Take time to review the seven principles below. What habits help or aide in your practice of the principles? What habits block you? For me, reminding myself of the truths of God help me practice principle one. When I focus on resentments toward leaders in my life, this makes me think of God in a negative light and hinders me from trusting him. To practice number two and four, I need to plan out time to study the Bible and sit in silence. I know that social media and staying up late block my practice. Limiting my social media time and going to bed early aide in my practice.

Think through your own habits and use the chart below to acknowledge the good and bad habits in your life right now. We saw David do these and thrive, how can we?

Principle	Good Habits That Aide	Bad Habits That Block
1. God Wants a Relationship With You		
2. Know Your Bible		
3. Know Your God		
4. Listening in the Silence		
5. The Posture of Humility and Submission		
6. Confess and Forgive		
7. Meditate on Truth		

In the apostle Paul's letter encouraging Timothy, Paul says,

> *"For this reason I remind you to fan into flame the gift of God, which is in you through the laying on of my hands, for God gave us a spirit not of fear but of power and love and self-control" (2 Tim. 1:6–7).*

We are each intentionally and specifically gifted by God. Being spiritually disciplined is how we combat fear and "fan into flame" the gifts God has given us. That is the power of forming these habits so we can run the race well, as Paul encouraged the Corinthians to do:

*"Every athlete exercises self-control in all things. They
do it to receive a perishable wreath, but we an
imperishable. So I do not run aimlessly; I do not box
as one beating the air. But I discipline my body and
keep it under control, lest after preaching to others I
myself should be disqualified"* (1 Cor. 9:25–27).

The disciplines laid out in this book are how I have learned to stay plugged in to God so I can thrive.

THRIVE

As I have been studying the topics of this book, God has been gracious to give me real life examples and analogies. One such analogy involves the two peach trees in my yard. When we planted them last year, they came with a nasty little disease that caused their leaves to wither and branches to break, preventing the production of fruit. Untended to, this disease would have killed our trees. However, our yard guy treated them and instructed me to prune the bad leaves and branches and make sure they got plenty of water.

Before our peach trees could thrive and produce fruit, they had to survive! The disease would have killed our trees before they ever produced a single juicy peach. Over time as the disease died the trees began to thrive. Their leaves looked healthy, there were no more brown spots or weird growths. The leaves became smooth and bright green and then fruit started to grow. It was a slow process, but I was consistent in my care, and we saw results.

The truth is that our individual thriving must start inside of us. In my analogy I was an outside force caring for the tree, but the reality is, we have the power to care for ourselves. My discipline in caring for the trees mirrors my own self-care. I must be diligent to remove the things in my life that cause me harm like bad habits, toxic relationships etc. Once I am healthy on the inside, I can start to produce fruit.

In the tree analogy, the season of work, before my trees produced fruit, is when I found myself being the most disciplined. I wanted to see fruit, so I worked hard every day doing the same maintenance, checking the soil, and cleaning away any dead leaves. This is the discipline and consistency we need in our spiritual lives, and what leads us to the next part— producing fruit that blesses us and others. Keep in mind that I am not saying that we need to work to earn salvation. Once we are saved, we are responsible for our growth, but God is right there tending to us. He will never leave us:

> *"And I am sure of this, that he who began a good work in you will bring it to completion at the day of Jesus Christ" (Philippians 1:6).*

HARDSHIP

After five years of being either pregnant or nursing, and then three years of parenting infants and toddlers I realized I was so focused on caring for three other humans that I had stopped taking care of myself. The kids literally sucked the life out of me. I was weak, exhausted, and not thriving physically. About a year ago I decided to make my physical health a priority. I signed up for a gym, started working with a trainer and attending workout classes. Finally, after a year I can say that I don't get tired at 2 pm, I have more mental clarity and emotional stability, and one of the biggest perks—I can play with my kids when they get home from school. I can run, play games, and I even have more patience with them.

Why am I telling you this? Yes, I was consistent with the habit of working out. Yes, I am healthier physically, mentally, and emotionally, and yes—I am a blessing to my kids because I have more energy. But I am telling you this because working out is freaking hard. It is not fun for me to lift heavy objects or push sleds or get into weird Pilates poses. My poor trainers have put up with me yelling at them and calling them mean and abusive. Some days after a workout I have to go home and lie down for an hour because it was so hard and painful. Other days I get migraines or flu-like symptoms.

I am telling you all this to say, to live a thriving Christian life that blesses others we have to endure the hard things. We are going to make mistakes, we are going to walk beside friends who are in horrible situations, we may even be in hard situations ourselves—cancer, abuse, divorce, financial troubles, rebellious seasons…they will all continue to happen around us and to us. Our thriving prayer life won't stop or prevent these things. But when we go to God in prayer during the hard times, keep working, fighting, loving, forgiving, and serving others—just like going to the gym every day—we will grow strong.

When the vine has to work hard to endure the sun's heat, the flavor is stronger. I recently toured a vineyard in California where I noticed that the earth around the vines was dry and sandy. The tour guide said that the irrigation has to be limited in order to keep from overwatering the grapes. When a vine struggles, the grapes are sweeter. A vine that gets too much water produces grapes that aren't as good and don't taste as sweet. We need consistency even when life is hard. Prayer and consistency are needed every day: on days when life is easy, on days when it is hard, when we are tired, when we are sad, and when we are happy.

David went through seasons of hardship when he was being chased by King Saul and later by his son Absalom, not to mention the battles he fought for the nation of Israel. (See 1 and 2 Samuel.) Growing grapes is tedious and difficult. They have to be watched and managed—I don't think God is unaware of what he is referencing in John 15.

We are difficult, but he is right there every day walking beside us and caring for us. Even when it's hard—he doesn't leave.

CONCLUSION

Life is difficult and walking with God isn't always easy but just like anyone training to do anything, you practice it every single day. Consistency is key—when you are tired, when you are angry, when you are sad and when you are happy. Prayer can change your life, but a life lived with discipline and consistency is where you'll see the true growth from these principles. God made you for the time and place that you are in (Acts 17:26) and he has a plan for you (Jeremiah 29:11). Don't you dare give up!

> "..we are what we repeatedly do. Excellence then is not an act but a habit..."

— WILL DURANT

1. Find 15 Minutes a Day Learning Something New.

CHAPTER 11

CONCLUSION

Dear Reader,

Thank you for spending the most valuable thing you have on reading this book: your time. I don't take it lightly and I pray this book blesses you exponentially.

I opened this book with a personal story about desperate prayer. I'd like to bring our discussion full circle here and close out with another look at praying desperately. There are two things most desperate prayers have in common: 1. An expectation that God will move and 2. A sense that the prayer is our absolute last resort.

Desperation happens when we are at the end of our logical ability to solve the problem. At this moment something amazing happens: we suspend our doubt long enough to hope. In Romans 5:5 God promises that even a small amount of "hope does not put us to shame, because God's love has been poured into our hearts through the Holy Spirit who has been given to us."

Desperation leads to hope. Another way of putting this is that hope leads to praying with expectation. When my child asks for dinner, she expects something. Desperate prayers expect something from God. Psalm 102:17 says,

> *"He regards the prayer of the destitute and does not*
> *despise their prayer."*

Another word for destitute is desperate. God is not annoyed with our desperation; he does not despise us. In fact, Mark 11:24 says,

> *"Therefore I tell you, whatever you ask in prayer,*
> *believe that you have received it, and it will be*
> *yours."*

The second part of desperate prayer is that it is usually our last resort. What if we changed this and made it the first resort in tackling our problems? For example, I have a favorite tea. I used to go from store to store trying different teas and you know what I learned? There are a lot of gross teas out there. Now I don't waste time going from store to store. When I run out, I go to HEB and buy my decaffeinated tranquil black mango tea. This principle applies to prayer as well. I no longer go to others for advice first. When I have a problem to solve, I go directly to the person who not only has the answer but also the power to fix any and every problem. I love the irony of the expression "It is always the last place you look" because of course it is! Once you find your lost item, you stop looking! So it is with prayer. Stop looking, you found the solution and it is at the foot of the throne of God. He is always listening and he is the one place where you can find all your answers and solutions. Psalm 147:5 says,

> *"Great is our Lord, and abundant in power; his under-*
> *standing is beyond measure."*

Another fun fact about me...I have a special skill. I can complicate the simplest of tasks by adding layers of emotion and stress that aren't in fact there. Prayer was no exception. For the longest time I thought prayer was for the pastor, the missionary, the spiritual elite who were all better than me. How complicated is that? When I started this journey in the ER all those years ago I felt like God showed me a picture of how I viewed prayer. He called it a "vending-machine relationship." He showed me that I viewed him the same way I viewed a vending machine. As many of you know, if you put money into a vending machine and then push the right buttons, whatever you want drops into your hands. That is how I viewed prayer. If I obeyed the rules, impressed others with my actions and prayed the right words, my prayers would be answered. Unfortunately, that meant the opposite was also true: if I don't do all the right things, I don't get what I ask for. This sterile, emotionless transaction is not what God has called me to do. He has called me (and you) into the same relationship my husband has with our daughter—a no exceptions, open-ended, always call, sit-in-his-lap relationship. It's simple; he wants to talk to you. Matthew 6:6 says, "But when you pray, go into your room and shut the door and pray to your Father who is in secret. And your Father who sees in secret will reward you." That is it. Pray like you are talking to your good father and he will see you and reward you. It is simple. Don't make it complicated.

I hope these seven simple principles help you to remove any complications or roadblocks you've encountered to effective prayer. I hope you discovered this book to be your invitation to have a relationship with the God of the Bible who loves you, chose you, and wants to talk to you. Humble yourself, find quiet, get to know God, confess your sins and forgive others. It's that simple. The reward? Well for me it started with greater joy than I could ever dream of, but the rewards for God's children are endless. For as 1 Corinthians 2:9 says,

*"No eye has seen, nor ear heard, nor the heart of man
imagined, what God has prepared for those who love
him."*

What will the reward be for you? I can't wait for you to find out. Please, accept this invitation, spend fifteen minutes a day on this habit and see if not only your life changes but also the lives of those for whom you pray.

The last thing I want to mention is something that we all know: we are at war right now. Scripture says that we are in a spiritual battle not "against flesh and blood, but against the rulers…authorities…the cosmic powers over this present darkness, against the spiritual forces of evil" (Ephesians 6:12). We are commanded to pray "at all times in the Spirit" (v. 18). Prayer is how we fight.

When I was researching for this book, I came across a story (sadly I can't find the source) about an enemy army going into battle against a Christian army. The Christian army had a group of ministers set up on a hill praying over the battle. The enemy army knew about the power of prayer so the commander ordered his troops to kill the ministers first. The enemy knows, arguably better than we, about the power of prayer. These seven principles not only give us joy and peace, but they will also keep us safe against our "adversary the devil [who] prowls around like a roaring lion, seeking someone to devour" (1 Peter 5:8). Through prayer we fight sin, battle for one another, and defend our minds.

To sum up: Come to God desperate, with expectation. Pray simply, don't make it complicated. And finally, no matter what obstacles you face, know that you can fight ANYTHING with prayer. When you pray, the God of the universe will hear you, come down from heaven and answer you.

Jeremiah 29:12–14a says,

"Then you will call upon me and come and pray to me, and I will hear you. You will seek me and find me, when you seek me with all your heart. I will be found by you, declares the LORD."

Be blessed my friends,

Lacey Rozell

ACKNOWLEDGMENTS

During my pregnancy with my son, bedridden and miserable, I started writing an outline of my beliefs on joy to remedy my desperation and depression. What started out as notes on finding joy soon turned into notes on prayer and were my motivation for writing a class on prayer. At the same time a prayer team was forming at our church, led by Josh and Audrie Patterson. What started as a common passion for seeing God's people learn to pray soon turned into Josh and I co-writing and teaching a class on prayer. We had a blast watching God work through the class as well as the prayer ministry at the Village Church Denton. Thank you, Josh, for our white board sessions, teaching back and forths and for removing stitches from two of my three children's faces.

Soon after writing and teaching the class, Scott and I felt called to leave Denton and move to NYC. In NYC my prayer life shifted in a new and challenging way, not only did I habitually practice these principles and pray all over the city, but the foundation of this class also led me to start writing Bible studies and workshops on prayer. NYC was where I finally decided to take the original prayer class, my Bible studies and workshops notes and turn them into a book. Soon I called on my sister-in-law and prayer partner Leanne Rozell who introduced me to my editor and coach Sarah Byrd. Sarah is one of those answered prayers where God gave me so much more than I could ever ask for, because I had no idea what to ask for. She has patiently coached me and prayed alongside me for the last two years. What a blessing her knowledge, experience and dedication has been. Which leads me to my next faithful sister-in-Christ, Lauren Simonic. Lauren is my diligent and gifted proof-reader whose red and yellow notes, though they kept me up at night, challenged and corrected me, making both me and this book better. Thank you Sarah and Lauren!

And to my husband and kids, thank you for praying for me, thank you for putting up with my strange writing hours and excessive sticky notes. Also for bringing these principles to life by always being the most interesting stories of God's love, compassion and faithfulness. Scott—you were my coach, cheerleader and shoulder to cry on. Thank you. I did this because of you.

ABOUT THE AUTHOR

Lacey Rozell is many things: mom of three, wife of one, native Texan, a blonde tornado, and co-owner of an education company with her husband. She spent years studying the topic of prayer before she dove head first into her call as a writer. This book is her story of God's powerful call for all of us to pray. From teaching in the classroom, to business ownership, church leadership, marriage and motherhood Lacey has prayed through it all in order to bring us this book on the power of prayer and the tools to enjoy God.

What if We Pray is her debut book based on over a decade of leading in church, writing a class on prayer and teaching prayer workshops at conferences. She hopes this book will encourage others in their relationship with God, and they will find new joy and peace in him.

You can stay up to date with Lacey on her website:

www.laceyrozell.com

Made in the USA
Columbia, SC
21 January 2025

51397292R00088